AF750805

RECENT ADVANCES IN DOCUMENT RECOGNITION AND UNDERSTANDING

Edited by **Minoru Mori**

Recent Advances in Document Recognition and Understanding
Edited by Minoru Mori

Published by InTech
Janeza Trdine 9, 51000 Rijeka, Croatia

Copyright © 2011 InTech
All chapters are distributed under the Creative Commons Attribution 3.0 license, which allows users to download, copy and build upon published articles even for commercial purposes, as long as the author and publisher are properly credited, which ensures maximum dissemination and a wider impact of our publications. After this work has been published by InTech, authors have the right to republish it, in whole or part, in any publication of which they are the author, and to make other personal use of the work. Any republication, referencing or personal use of the work must explicitly identify the original source.

As for readers, this license allows users to download, copy and build upon published chapters even for commercial purposes, as long as the author and publisher are properly credited, which ensures maximum dissemination and a wider impact of our publications.

Notice
Statements and opinions expressed in the chapters are these of the individual contributors and not necessarily those of the editors or publisher. No responsibility is accepted for the accuracy of information contained in the published chapters. The publisher assumes no responsibility for any damage or injury to persons or property arising out of the use of any materials, instructions, methods or ideas contained in the book.

Publishing Process Manager Niksa Mandic

Technical Editor Teodora Smiljanic

Cover Designer InTech Design Team

Additional hard copies can be obtained from orders@intechopen.com

Recent Advances in Document Recognition and Understanding, Edited by Minoru Mori
p. cm.
ISBN 978-953-307-320-0

We are IntechOpen, the world's leading publisher of Open Access books

Built by scientists, for scientists

4,000+
Open access books available

116,000+
International authors and editors

120M+
Downloads

151
Countries delivered to

Our authors are among the
Top 1%
most cited scientists

12.2%
Contributors from top 500 universities

CLARIVATE ANALYTICS
BOOK CITATION INDEX
INDEXED

WEB OF SCIENCE™

Selection of our books indexed in the Book Citation Index in Web of Science™ Core Collection (BKCI)

Interested in publishing with us?
Contact book.department@intechopen.com

Numbers displayed above are based on latest data collected.
For more information visit www.intechopen.com

For EU product safety concerns:
IN TECH d.o.o., Prolaz Marije Krucifikse Kozulić 3, 51000 Rijeka, Croatia,
info@intechopen.com or visit our website at intechopen.com.

Meet the editor

Dr. Minoru Mori received the B.E. and Ph.D. degrees in electrical engineering from Tokyo Institute of Technology in 1993 and 2008, respectively. In 1993, he joined Nippon Telegraph and Telephone (NTT). He was engaged in developing character recognition and Image processing systems. He was an assistant manager in Broadband Business Development Division of NTT-East Corp. from 2003 to 2006 and a manager in NTT Advanced Technology Corp. from 2006 to 2007. Since 2007, he has been an senior research scientist in NTT Communication Science Laboratories. He was also an assistant professor of IREIIMS of Tokyo Women's Medical University from 2008 to 2010. His interests include document analysis, pattern recognition, and image processing. He is a senior member of IEICE.

Contents

Preface

In the field of document recognition and understanding, whereas scanned paper documents were previously the only recognition target, various new media such as camera-captured documents, videos, and natural scene images have recently started to attract attention because of the growth of the Internet/WWW and the rapid adoption of low-priced digital cameras/videos. The keys to the breakthrough include character detection from complex backgrounds, discrimination of characters from non-characters, modern or ancient unique font recognition, fast retrieval technique from large-scaled scanned documents, multi-lingual OCR, and unconstrained handwriting recognition. This book aims to present recent advances, applications, and new ideas that are relevant to document recognition and understanding, from technical topics such as image processing, feature extraction or classification, to new applications like camera-based recognition or character-based natural scene analysis. The goal of this book is to provide a new trend and a reference source for academic research and for professionals working in the document recognition and understanding field.

Minoru Mori
NTT Communication Science Laboratories, NTT Corp.,
Japan

1

Statistical Deformation Model for Handwritten Character Recognition

Seiichi Uchida
Kyushu University
Japan

1. Introduction

One of the main problems of offline and online handwritten character recognition is how to deal with the deformations in characters. A promising strategy to this problem is the incorporation of a deformation model. If recognition can be done with a reasonable deformation model, it may become tolerant to deformations within each character category.

There have been proposed many deformation models and some of them were designed in an empirical manner. Recognition methods based on elastic matching have often relied on a continuous and monotonic deformation model (Bahlmann & Burkhardt, 2004; Burr, 1983; Connell & Jain, 2001; Fujimoto et al., 1976; Yoshida & Sakoe, 1982). This is a typical empirical model and has been developed according to the observation that character patterns often preserve their topologies. Affine deformation models (Wakahara, 1994; Wakahara & Odaka, 1997; Wakahara et al., 2001) and local perturbation models (or image distortion models (Keysers et al., 2004)) are also popular empirical deformation models.

While the empirical models generally work well in handwritten character recognition tasks, they are not well-grounded by actual deformations of handwritten characters. In addition, the empirical models are just approximations of actual deformations and they cannot incorporate category-dependent deformation characteristics. In fact, the category-dependent deformation characteristics exist. For example, in category "M", two parallel vertical strokes are often slanted to be closer. In contrast, in category "H", however, the same deformation is rarely observed.

Statistical models are better alternatives to the empirical models. The statistical models learn deformation characteristics from actual character patterns. Thus, if a model learns the deformations of a certain category, it can represent the category-dependent deformation characteristics.

Hidden Markov model (HMM) is a popular statistical model for handwritten characters (e.g., (Cho et al., 1995; Hu et al., 1996; Kuo & Agazzi, 1994; Nag et al., 1986; Nakai et al., 2001; Park & Lee, 1998)). HMM has not only a solid stochastic background and but also a well-established learning scheme. HMM, however, has a limitation on regulating global deformation characteristics; that is, HMM can regulate local deformations of neighboring regions due to its Markovian property.

This chapter is concerned with another statistical deformation model of offline and online handwritten characters. This deformation model is based on a combination of elastic matching and principal component analysis (PCA) and also capable of learning actual deformations of

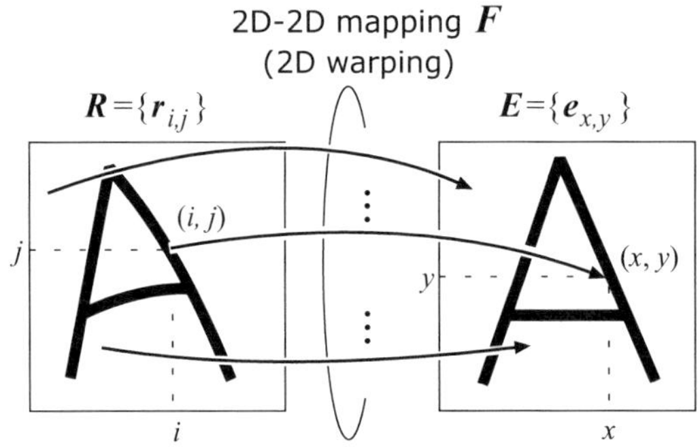

Fig. 1. Elastic matching between two character images.

handwritten characters. Different from HMM, this deformation model can regulate not only local deformations but also global deformations. In the following, the contributions of this chapter are summarized.

1.1 Contributions of this chapter

The first contribution of this chapter is to introduce a statistical deformation model for *offline* handwritten character recognition. The model is realized by two steps. The first step is the automatic extraction of the deformations of character images by elastic matching. Elastic matching is formulated as an optimization problem of the pixel-to-pixel correspondence between two image patterns. Since the resulting pixel-to-pixel correspondence represents the displacement of individual pixels, i.e., the deformation of one character image from another. The second step is statistical analysis of the extracted deformations by PCA. The resulting principal components, called *eigen-deformations*, represent intrinsic deformations of handwritten characters.

The second contribution is to introduce a statistical deformation model for *online* handwritten character recognition. While the discussion is similar to the above offline case, it is different in several points. For example, deformations often appear as the difference in pattern length. Consequently, online handwritten character patterns have rarely been handled in a PCA-based statistical analysis framework, which assumes the same dimensionality of subjected patterns. In addition, online handwritten character patterns often undergo heavy nonlinear temporal/spatial fluctuation. Elastic matching to extract the relative deformation between two patterns solves these problems and helps to establish a statistical deformation model.

2. Statistical deformation model of offline handwritten character recognition

2.1 Extraction of deformations by elastic matching

The first step for statistical deformation analysis of handwritten character images is the extraction of deformations of actual handwritten character images and it can be done automatically by elastic matching. Elastic matching is formulated as the following optimization problem. Consider an $I \times I$ reference character image $\boldsymbol{R} = \{\boldsymbol{r}_{i,j}\}$ and an $I \times I$ input character image $\boldsymbol{E} = \{\boldsymbol{e}_{x,y}\}$, where $\boldsymbol{r}_{i,j}$ and $\boldsymbol{e}_{x,y}$ are d-dimensional pixel feature vectors at pixel (i,j) on $\boldsymbol{R}$ and (x,y) on $\boldsymbol{E}$, respectively. Let $\boldsymbol{F}$ denote a 2D-2D mapping from $\boldsymbol{R}$ to $\boldsymbol{E}$, i.e., $\boldsymbol{F} : (i,j) \mapsto (x,y)$. As shown in Figure 1, the mapping $\boldsymbol{F}$ determines the

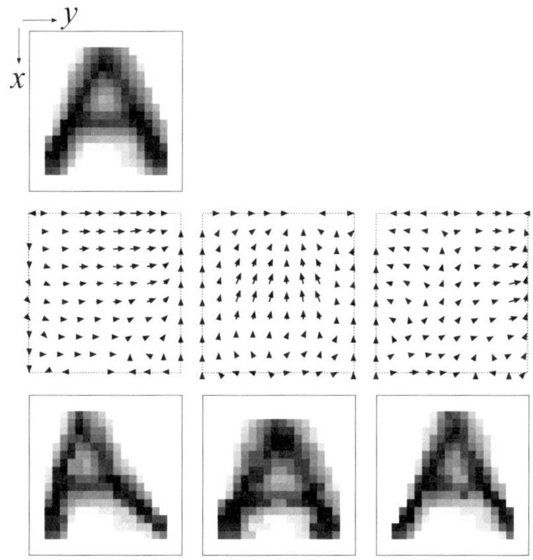

Fig. 2. Eigen-deformations of handwritten characters.

pixel-to-pixel correspondence from $\boldsymbol{R}$ to $\boldsymbol{E}$. Elastic matching between $\boldsymbol{R}$ and $\boldsymbol{E}$ is formulated as the minimization problem of the following objective function with respect to $\boldsymbol{F}$:

$$J_{\boldsymbol{R},\boldsymbol{E}}(\boldsymbol{F}) = \|\boldsymbol{R} - \boldsymbol{E}_{\boldsymbol{F}}\|, \tag{1}$$

where $\boldsymbol{E}_{\boldsymbol{F}}$ is the character image obtained by fitting $\boldsymbol{E}$ to $\boldsymbol{R}$, i.e., $\boldsymbol{E}_{\boldsymbol{F}} = \{\boldsymbol{e}_{x_{i,j},y_{i,j}}\}$, and $(x_{i,j}, y_{i,j})$ denotes the pixel of $\boldsymbol{E}$ corresponding to the (i,j)th pixel of $\boldsymbol{R}$ under $\boldsymbol{F}$. On the minimization, several constraints (such as a smoothness constraint and boundary constraints) are often assumed to regularize $\boldsymbol{F}$.

Let $\tilde{\boldsymbol{F}}$ denote the mapping $\boldsymbol{F}$ which minimizes $J_{\boldsymbol{R},\boldsymbol{E}}(\boldsymbol{F})$ of (1). This mapping $\tilde{\boldsymbol{F}}$ represents the relative deformation of the input image $\boldsymbol{E}$ from the reference image $\boldsymbol{R}$. Specifically, the deformation of $\boldsymbol{E}$ is extracted as the following $2I^2$-dimensional vector, called *deformation vector*,

$$\boldsymbol{v} = ((1 - x_{1,1}, 1 - y_{1,1}), \ldots, (i - x_{i,j}, j - y_{i,j}), \ldots, (I - x_{I,I}, I - y_{I,I}))^T. \tag{2}$$

Note that $\boldsymbol{v}$ is a discrete representation of $\tilde{\boldsymbol{F}}$.

The constrained minimization of (1) with respect to $\boldsymbol{F}$ (i.e., the extraction of $\boldsymbol{v}$) is done by various optimization strategies. If the mapping $\boldsymbol{F}$ is defined as a parametric function, iterative strategies and exhaustive strategies are often employed for optimizing the parameters of $\boldsymbol{F}$. In contrast, if the mapping $\boldsymbol{F}$ is a non-parametric function, combinatorial optimization strategies, such as dynamic programming, local perturbation, and deterministic relaxation, are employed. Various formulations and optimization strategies of the elastic matching problem are summarized in Uchida & Sakoe (2005).

2.2 Estimations of eigen-deformations

Eigen-deformations of a category are intrinsic deformations of the category and defined as M principal axes $\{\boldsymbol{u}_1, \ldots, \boldsymbol{u}_m, \ldots, \boldsymbol{u}_M\}$ which span an M-dimensional subspace in the $2I^2$-dimensional deformation space. The eigen-deformations can be estimated by applying

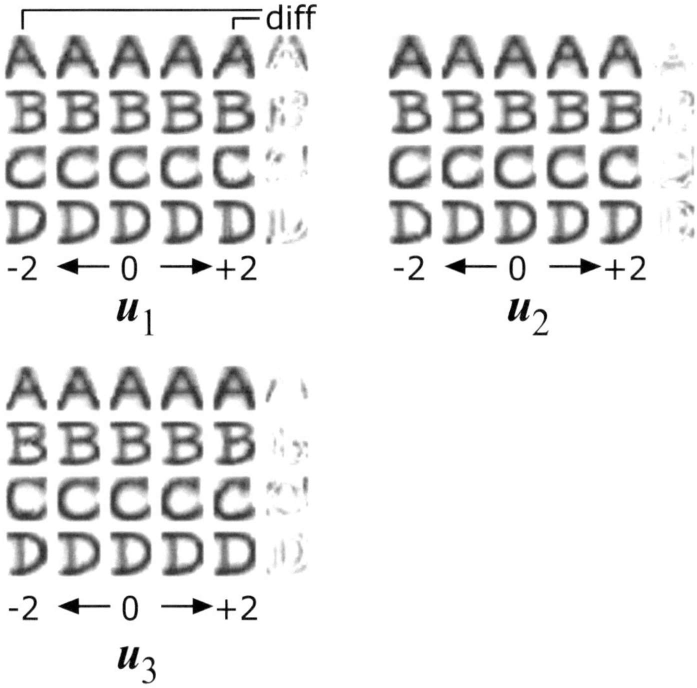

Fig. 3. Reference pattern $\boldsymbol{R}$ deformed by top three eigen-deformations, $\boldsymbol{u}_1$, $\boldsymbol{u}_2$, and $\boldsymbol{u}_3$.

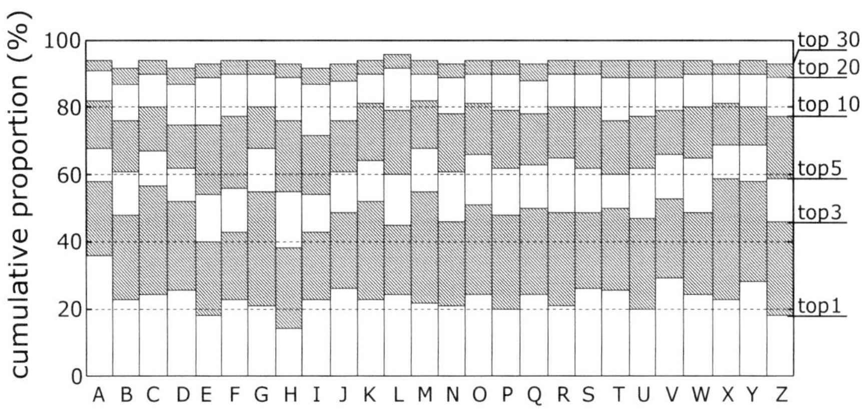

Fig. 4. Category-wise cumulative proportion $\rho(M)$ of eigen-deformations at $M = 1, 3, 5, 10, 20$, and 30. Note that $\rho(M) = 100\%$ at $M = 74$.

PCA to $\{\boldsymbol{v}_n | n = 1, \ldots, N\}$, where $\boldsymbol{v}_n$ is the extracted deformation between $\boldsymbol{R}$ and $\boldsymbol{E}_n$. Specifically, the eigen-deformations are obtained as the eigen-vectors of the covariance matrix $\Sigma = \sum_n (\boldsymbol{v}_n - \overline{\boldsymbol{v}})(\boldsymbol{v}_n - \overline{\boldsymbol{v}})^T / N$, where $\overline{\boldsymbol{v}}$ is the mean vector of $\{\boldsymbol{v}_n\}$.
Figure 2 shows the first three eigen-deformations estimated from 500 handwritten characters of the category "A". The first eigen-deformation $\boldsymbol{u}_1$, that is, the most frequent deformation of "A", was the global slant transformation. The second was the vertical shift of the horizontal

stroke and the third was the width variation of the upper part. Consequently, this figure confirms that frequent deformations of "A" were extracted successfully.
Note that in this experiment, the dimensionality of the deformation vector $\boldsymbol{v}$ was 74 though the size of the character image pattern was 20×20 (i.e., $I = 20$ and $2I^2 = 800$). This is because a "sparse" EM was used where the displacements of 3 pixels (leftmost, middle, and rightmost) were optimized at every row. The displacements of the other pixels were given by linear interpolation.
Figure 3 shows the patterns $\boldsymbol{R}$ deformed by the first three eigen-deformations $\boldsymbol{u}_1$, $\boldsymbol{u}_2$, and $\boldsymbol{u}_3$ with the amplification with $k\sqrt{\lambda_m}$ ($k = -2, -1, 0, 1, 2$), where λ_m is the eigenvalue of the mth eigenvector. This figure also show that frequent deformations were extracted as the eigen-deformation at each category.
Figure 4 shows the cumulative proportion of each category. The cumulative proportion by the top M eigen-deformations is defined as $\rho(M) = \sum_{m=1}^{M} \lambda_m / \sum_{m=1}^{74} \lambda_m$. In all categories, the cumulative proportion exceeded 50% with the top $3 \sim 5$ eigen-deformations and 80% with the top $10 \sim 20$ eigen-deformations. Thus, the distribution of deformation vectors was not isotropic and can be approximated by a small number of eigen-deformations. In other words, there existed a low-dimensional and efficient subspace of deformations.

2.3 Recognition with eigen-deformations (1)

The eigen-deformations can be utilized for recognizing handwritten character images. A direct use of the eigen-deformations for evaluating a distance between two characters $\boldsymbol{R}$ and $\boldsymbol{E}$ is as follows:

$$D_{\text{disp}}(\boldsymbol{R}, \boldsymbol{E}) = (\boldsymbol{v} - \overline{\boldsymbol{v}})^T \Sigma^{-1} (\boldsymbol{v} - \overline{\boldsymbol{v}}) = \sum_{m=1}^{2I^2} \frac{1}{\lambda_m} \langle \boldsymbol{v} - \overline{\boldsymbol{v}}, \boldsymbol{u}_m \rangle^2, \tag{3}$$

where $\boldsymbol{E}$ is an unknown input image and $\boldsymbol{v}$ is the deformation extracted by the elastic matching between $\boldsymbol{R}$ and $\boldsymbol{E}$. This is the well-known Mahalanobis distance and evaluates the statistical divergence of the estimated deformation on $\boldsymbol{E}$ from the deformations which usually appear in the category of $\boldsymbol{R}$. If the estimated deformation $\boldsymbol{v}$ gives a large distance value, the result of elastic matching between $\boldsymbol{E}$ and $\boldsymbol{R}$ is somewhat abnormal and therefore the category of $\boldsymbol{R}$ will not become a candidate of the correct category of $\boldsymbol{E}$.
The recognition performance by $D_{\text{disp}}(\boldsymbol{R}, \boldsymbol{E})$ alone, however, is not satisfactory. This is because the distance $D_{\text{disp}}(\boldsymbol{R}, \boldsymbol{E})$ completely neglects the distance of pixel features. This fact will be certified through an experimental result in 2.5.
An alternative and reasonable choice is the linear combination of the distance in the pixel feature space and the distance in the deformation space (Uchida & Sakoe, 2003b), that is,

$$D_{\text{hybrid}}(\boldsymbol{R}, \boldsymbol{E}) = (1 - w) D_{\text{feat}}(\boldsymbol{R}, \boldsymbol{E}) + w D_{\text{disp}}(\boldsymbol{R}, \boldsymbol{E}), \tag{4}$$

where $D_{\text{feat}}(\boldsymbol{R}, \boldsymbol{E})$ is the elastic matching distance in the pixel feature space, i.e.,

$$D_{\text{feat}}(\boldsymbol{R}, \boldsymbol{E}) = J_{\boldsymbol{R},\boldsymbol{E}}(\tilde{\boldsymbol{F}}), \tag{5}$$

and w is a constant ($0 \le w \le 1$) to ballance two distances.
In practice, the modified Mahalanobis distance (Kimura et al., 1987) is employed instead of (3). Specifically, the higher-order eigenvalues λ_m ($m = M + 2, \ldots, 2I^2$) are replaced by

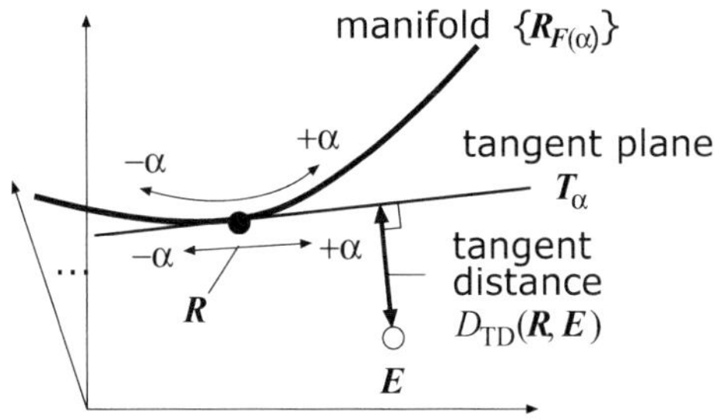

Fig. 5. Manifold $\boldsymbol{R}_\alpha$, its tangent plane $\boldsymbol{T}_\alpha$, and tangent distance $D_{\text{TD}}(\boldsymbol{R}, \boldsymbol{E})$.

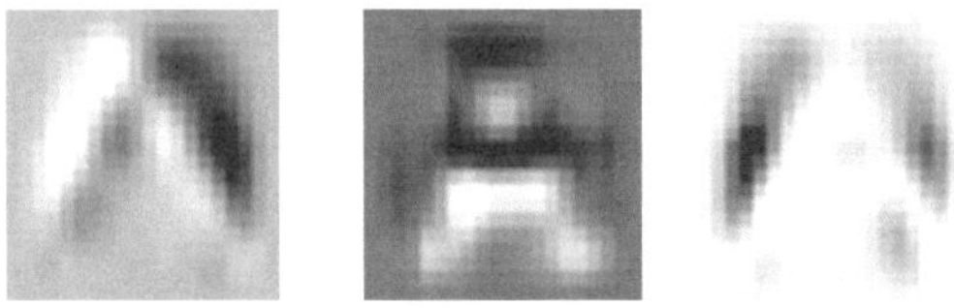

Fig. 6. Tangent vectors of the category "A", derived from $\boldsymbol{R}$ and eigen-deformations $\boldsymbol{u}_1$, $\boldsymbol{u}_2$, and $\boldsymbol{u}_3$.

λ_{M+1}, to suppress the estimation errors of higher-order eigenvalues in (3). According to this replacement, (3) is reduced to

$$D_{\text{disp}}(\boldsymbol{R}, \boldsymbol{E}) \sim \frac{1}{\lambda_{M+1}} \|\boldsymbol{v} - \overline{\boldsymbol{v}}\| + \sum_{m=1}^{M} \left(\frac{1}{\lambda_m} - \frac{1}{\lambda_{M+1}} \right) \langle \boldsymbol{v} - \overline{\boldsymbol{v}}, \boldsymbol{u}_m \rangle^2. \tag{6}$$

The parameter M is to be determined experimentally, for example, considering the cumulative proportion $\rho(M)$.

2.4 Recognition with eigen-deformations (2)

The above recognition method has a weak-point that two heterogeneous distances D_{feat} and D_{disp} are added naively to create the single distance D_{hybrid}. In contrast, the following method (Uchida & Sakoe, 2003a) can avoid this weak-point by embedding the eigen-deformations into an elastic matching procedure.

Consider that the mapping $\boldsymbol{F}$ is defined as a linear combination of eigen-deformations, i.e.,

$$\boldsymbol{F}(\alpha) = \sum_{m=1}^{M} \alpha_m \boldsymbol{u}_m, \tag{7}$$

where $\alpha = (\alpha_1, \ldots, \alpha_m, \ldots, \alpha_M)^T$. Then an elastic matching problem with $\boldsymbol{F}(\alpha)$ can be formulated as the minimization problem of the following objective function:

$$J_{\boldsymbol{R},\boldsymbol{E}}(\alpha) = \left\| \boldsymbol{R}_{\boldsymbol{F}(\alpha)} - \boldsymbol{E} \right\|, \tag{8}$$

where $\boldsymbol{R}_{\boldsymbol{F}(\alpha)}$ is the reference pattern deformed by the mapping $\boldsymbol{F}(\alpha)$.

The set of deformed reference patterns, $\{\boldsymbol{R}_{\boldsymbol{F}(\alpha)} | \forall \alpha\}$, will form an M-dimensional manifold in an $(I^2 \cdot d)$-dimensional pixel feature space. Thus the minimum value of $J_{\boldsymbol{R},\boldsymbol{E}}(\alpha)$ is equivalent to the shortest distance between the M-dimensional manifold and $\boldsymbol{E}$.

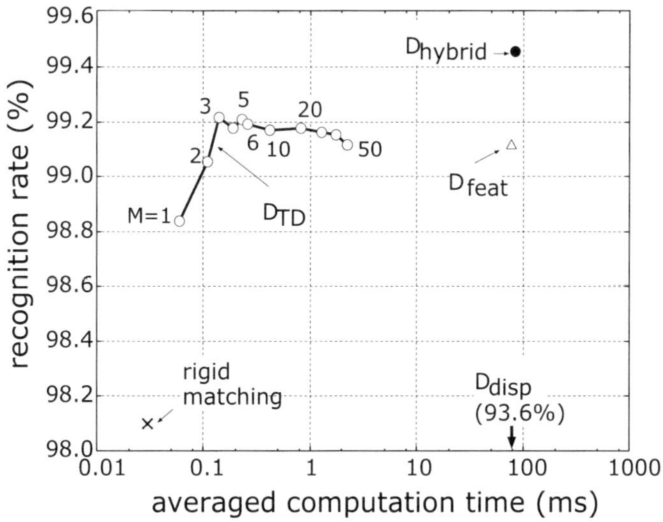

Fig. 7. Relation between computation time (ms) and recognition rate (%).

The minimization problem (8) with respect to α is hard to solve directly. This is because the M-dimensional parameter vector α to be optimized is involved in the nonlinear function $\boldsymbol{R}$. Thus, some approximation is required to solve the optimization problem.

In Uchida & Sakoe (2003a), the approximation scheme used in the tangent distance method (Simard et al., 1992) has been employed for the above minimization problem. As shown in Fig. 5, the minimum distance $\min_\alpha J_{\boldsymbol{R},\boldsymbol{E}}(\alpha)$ can be approximated by the following *tangent distance*,

$$D_{\mathrm{TD}}(\boldsymbol{R}, \boldsymbol{E}) = \min_{\alpha} \|\boldsymbol{T}_\alpha - \boldsymbol{E}\|, \tag{9}$$

where $\boldsymbol{T}_\alpha$ is the tangent plane of the manifold at $\alpha = 0$. The tangent plane is an M-dimensional hyperplane in the feature space and linear with respect to α. Thus the minimization problem of (9) has a closed-form solution. Intuitively speaking, the distance $D_{\mathrm{TD}}(\boldsymbol{R}, \boldsymbol{E})$ is the Euclidean distance between the input $\boldsymbol{E}$ and its closest point on the tangent plane. Figure 6 shows three tangent vectors which span the tangent plane of the category "A".

2.5 Recognition result

Figure 7 shows results of a handwritten character recognition experiment using 26 (categories) $\times$ 1,100 (samples) isolated handwritten English uppercase character images from the standard character image database ETL6. The first 100 samples of each category were simply averaged to create one reference pattern $\boldsymbol{R}$ and the next 500 samples were used as training samples $\boldsymbol{E}_n$ to estimate the eigen-deformations. The remaining 500 samples ($13,000 = 26 \times 500$ samples in total) were used as test samples $\boldsymbol{E}$.

The highest recognition rate (99.47%) was attained by D_{hybrid} with its best weight w. The recognition rate by D_{disp}, i.e., the recognition rate by evaluating only the deformation $\boldsymbol{v}$, was not sufficient. Thus, the pixel features (i.e., appearance features) should not be neglected for evaluating the distance of two character images. The recognition rates by D_{TD} were saturated around $M = 3$. This result is supported by the fast saturation of the cumulative proportion of Fig. 4.

2.6 Related work

The original idea of the eigen-deformations, i.e., principal components of deformations, can be found in the point distribution models (PDM), which has been proposed by Cootes et al. (1995) and applied to various patterns. Shen & Davatzikos (2000) have introduced an automatic deformation collection scheme into the PDM. PDM for curvilinear patterns has been applied to face recognition (Lanitis et al., 1997), Chinese character recognition (Shi et al., 2003), and hand posture recognition (Ahmed et al., 1997). Uchida & Sakoe (2003b) have extended the PDM to deal with fully 2D deformations and have applied to an elastic matching-based handwritten character recognition system.

Iwai et al. (1997) have applied PCA to interframe motion vector fields obtained by block matching, which can be considered as the simplest elastic matching. Bing et al (2002) have proposed a face expression recognition method based on a subspace of face deformations. Naster et al. (1997) have analyzed a deformation vector extended to deal with the variation of the pixel feature value. Those ideas will be promising for recognizing handwritten character images.

The eigen-deformations are the principal axes spanning a subspace of the $2I^2$-dimensional deformation space. Any point on the subspace represents a deformation $\boldsymbol{F}$. On the other hands, we can consider a subspace on the $(I^2 \cdot d)$-dimensional pixel feature space. Any point on the subspace represents an $I \times I \times d$ image pattern. The axes spanning this subspace are derived as dominant eigen-vectors of the covariance matrix $\Sigma = \sum_n (\boldsymbol{E}_n - \overline{\boldsymbol{E}})(\boldsymbol{E}_n - \overline{\boldsymbol{E}})^T / N$, where $\overline{\boldsymbol{E}}$ is the mean vector of $\{\boldsymbol{E}_n\}$. There are huge research attempts about the subspace (Oja, 1983). Eigenface (Turk & Pentland, 1991) and parametric eigenspace (Hase et al., 2003; Murase & Nayar, 1994) are famous examples of those attempts. While the subspace derived in the above manner can represent a set of deformed character patterns, the subspace spanned by the eigen-deformations will represent the same set in a more compact manner. Consider a character image $\boldsymbol{R}$ and a set of character images created by translating $\boldsymbol{R}$. The number of the eigen-deformations estimated from the set is two; one will represent horizontal shift and the other vertical shift. In contrast, the number of the principal eigen-vectors in the pixel feature space will be far larger than two. This superiority will hold for other geometric deformations and thus the subspace of deformations can be a more efficient representation than the subspace of the pixel features.

3. Statistical deformation model of online handwritten character recognition

3.1 Extraction of deformations by elastic matching

Consider two online handwritten character patterns, $\boldsymbol{R} = \boldsymbol{r}_1, \boldsymbol{r}_2, \ldots, \boldsymbol{r}_i, \ldots, \boldsymbol{r}_I$ and $\boldsymbol{E} = \boldsymbol{e}_1, \boldsymbol{e}_2, \ldots, \boldsymbol{e}_x, \ldots, \boldsymbol{e}_{I'}$. The former is a reference character pattern and the latter is an input character pattern. Their elements $\boldsymbol{r}_i$ and $\boldsymbol{e}_x$ are d-dimensional feature vectors representing the features at i and x; they are often 3-dimensional vectors comprised of x-coordinate, y-coordinate, and local direction.

Let $\boldsymbol{F}$ denote a 1D-1D mapping from $\boldsymbol{R}$ to $\boldsymbol{E}$, i.e., $\boldsymbol{F} : i \mapsto x$. Figure 8 depicts $\boldsymbol{F}$. Elastic matching between $\boldsymbol{R}$ and $\boldsymbol{E}$ is formulated as the minimization of the following objective function with respect to $\boldsymbol{F}$,

$$J_{\boldsymbol{R},\boldsymbol{E}}(\boldsymbol{F}) = \|\boldsymbol{R} - \boldsymbol{E}_{\boldsymbol{F}}\|, \tag{10}$$

where $\boldsymbol{E}_{\boldsymbol{F}}$ is the character pattern obtained by fitting $\boldsymbol{E}$ to $\boldsymbol{R}$, i.e., $\boldsymbol{E}_{\boldsymbol{F}} = \boldsymbol{e}_{x_1}, \ldots, \boldsymbol{e}_{x_i}, \ldots, \boldsymbol{e}_{x_I}$, where x_i represents the $i - x$ correspondence under $\boldsymbol{F}$. On the minimization, several

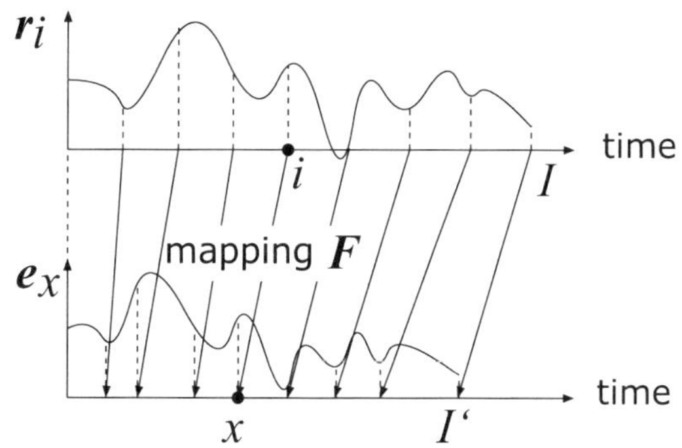

Fig. 8. Elastic matching between two online handwritten character patterns.

constraints (such as the monotonicity and continuity constraint defined as $x_i - x_{i-1} \in \{0,1,2\}$ and boundary constraints $x_1 = 1$ and $x_I = I'$) are often assumed to regularize $\boldsymbol{F}$. This constrained minimization problem can be solved effectively by a DP algorithm, called dynamic time warping or DP matching, and its detail are omitted here.

The deformation of $\boldsymbol{E}$ from $\boldsymbol{R}$ is represented by the following $(I \cdot d)$-dimensional deformation vector,

$$\boldsymbol{v} = \left(\boldsymbol{e}_{x_1} - \boldsymbol{r}_1, \ldots, \boldsymbol{e}_{x_i} - \boldsymbol{r}_i, \ldots, \boldsymbol{e}_{x_I} - \boldsymbol{r}_I\right)^T . \tag{11}$$

It should be noted that the dimension of the above deformation vector $\boldsymbol{v}$ is fixed at $(I \cdot d)$ and independent of the length of $\boldsymbol{E}$, i.e., I'. This property is very important to apply various statistical methods, such as PCA, to sequential patterns.

Also note that it is possible to define $\boldsymbol{v}$ as

$$\boldsymbol{v} = \left(1 - x_1, \ldots, i - x_i, \ldots, I - x_I\right)^T .$$

Although this definition is a straightforward modification of the deformation vector of (2), we will use $\boldsymbol{v}$ of (11) as a deformation vector here. This is because in online character recognition, $\boldsymbol{r}_i$ and $\boldsymbol{e}_x$ are often spatial features and thus their difference represents a deformation.

3.2 Estimation of eigen-deformations

Eigen-deformations of online handwritten character patterns are also estimated by the procedure of 2.2; that is, they can be estimated as dominant eigen-vectors of the covariance matrix of $\boldsymbol{v}$.

Eigen-deformations of online handwritten digits were estimated by using about 1,000 samples from UNIPEN Train-R01/V07 database (1a) (Guyon et al., 1994). Figure 9 shows character patterns generated by $\boldsymbol{R} + \overline{\boldsymbol{v}} \pm 2\sqrt{\lambda_m}\boldsymbol{u}_m$ $(m = 1,2)$ (Mitoma et al., 2005). That is, those patterns are reference patterns deformed by their mean deformation vector $\overline{\boldsymbol{v}}$ and the first two eigen-deformations $\boldsymbol{u}_m$. Note that the effect of $\overline{\boldsymbol{v}}$ was not significant because $\boldsymbol{R}$ was set around the center of the set of the training samples by a clustering technique and thus the norm of $\overline{\boldsymbol{v}}$ was small.

Figure 9 shows that deformations frequently observed in actual characters were estimated as eigen-deformations. For example, the first eigen-deformation of "6" represents the vertical variation of its loop part, and the second one represents the horizontal variation of the loop part.

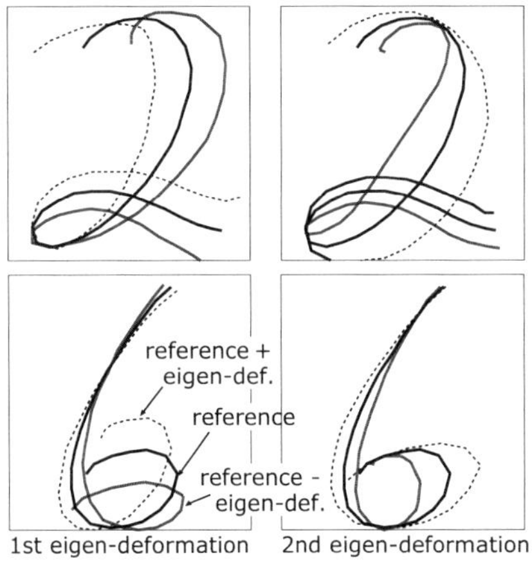

Fig. 9. Reference character pattern deformed by the first two eigen-deformations of "2" and "6".

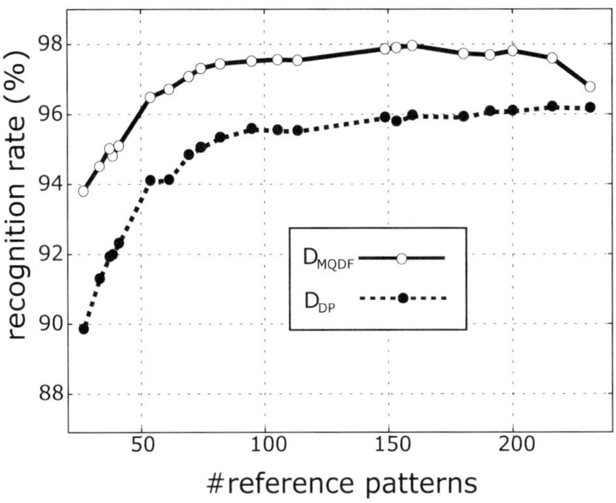

Fig. 10. Accuracy of online character recognition based on eigen-deformations.

3.3 Recognition with eigen-deformations

For online handwritten character recognition based on the eigen-deformations, the following quadratic discrimination function (QDF) is a possible choice (Mitoma et al., 2005). The QDF is the Bayes discrimination function under the assumption that the deformation vectors have a Gaussian distribution and defined as

$$D_{\text{QDF}}(\boldsymbol{R}, \boldsymbol{E}) = (\boldsymbol{v} - \overline{\boldsymbol{v}})^T \Sigma^{-1} (\boldsymbol{v} - \overline{\boldsymbol{v}}) + \log |\Sigma| + (I \cdot d) \log 2\pi$$
$$= \sum_{m=1}^{I \cdot d} \frac{1}{\lambda_m} \langle \boldsymbol{v} - \overline{\boldsymbol{v}}, \boldsymbol{u}_m \rangle^2 + \log \prod_{m=1}^{I \cdot d} \lambda_m + (I \cdot d) \log 2\pi. \quad (12)$$

The last term, $(I \cdot d) \log 2\pi$, cannot be omitted here because each category has a different dimension of $\boldsymbol{v}$ (i.e., $I \cdot d$).

As noted 2.3, the estimation errors of higher-order eigenvalues are amplified in (12). Thus, the modified quadratic discriminant function (MQDF) (Kimura et al., 1987) was employed, where the higher-order eigenvalues λ_m $(m = M+1, \ldots, I \cdot d)$ are replaced by λ_{M+1}, i.e.,

$$D_{\mathrm{MQDF}}(\boldsymbol{R}_c, \boldsymbol{E}) \sim \frac{1}{\lambda_{M+1}} \|\boldsymbol{v} - \overline{\boldsymbol{v}}\|^2 + \sum_{m=1}^{M} \left(\frac{1}{\lambda_m} - \frac{1}{\lambda_{M+1}} \right) \langle \boldsymbol{v} - \overline{\boldsymbol{v}}, \boldsymbol{u}_m \rangle^2$$
$$+ \log \left\{ (\lambda_{M+1})^{I \cdot d - M} \prod_{m=1}^{M} \lambda_m \right\} + (I \cdot d) \log 2\pi. \tag{13}$$

The parameter M is to be determined experimentally.

3.4 Recognition results

Figure 10 shows the results of an online character recognition experiment using digit samples from the UNIPEN database. Recognition rates attained by D_{MQDF} are plotted as a function of the total number of reference patterns, which are created by a clustering technique. The recognition rates attained by the conventional DP-matching distance (D_{DP}), which equals to the minimum value of (10), are also plotted.

As shown in Fig. 10, MQDF with the eigen-deformations outperformed the DP-matching distance. This will be because elastic matching results $\boldsymbol{F}$ which were deviated from the distribution of the deformations of the category were penalized by the eigen-deformations in MQDF. Thus, the above recognition method can avoid misrecognitions due to overfitting, which is the phenomenon that the distance between $\boldsymbol{E}$ and $\boldsymbol{R}$ of a wrong category is underestimated by unnatural mapping $\boldsymbol{F}$.

This result also proves that D_{MQDF} outperforms that statistical dynamic time warping (SDTW) (Bahlmann & Burkhardt, 2004), which is a recent and sophisticated online character recognition technique. In fact, it has been reported in Bahlmann & Burkhardt (2004) that SDTW attained 97.10% on the same UNIPEN data set by 150 reference patterns.

3.5 Related work

Sequential patterns, such as online handwritten character patterns, are often re-sampled to have the same dimension in advance to applying PCA or other statistical analysis techniques. For example, Deepu et al. (2004) have proposed an online character recognition technique based on a subspace method where all online character patterns are re-sampled to have a constant number of data points. The online character recognition technique by Zheng et al. (1999) is more radical because they used only two points (i.e., the start point and the end point) for each character stroke segment. In the handwriting synthesis technique by Wang et al. (2005), online cursive handwritings are firstly aligned to be the same dimension and then PCA is applied to them. PCA-based gesture/motion analysis techniques (Fod et al., 2002; Sanger, 1995; Yacoob & Black, 1999) also re-sampled gesture patterns to have the same dimension. An exception is Martens & Claesen (1996), which employed elastic matching to extract a fixed-dimensional deformation vector from online signatures.

4. Conclusion

Statistical deformation models of handwritten character images and online handwritten character patterns have been introduced. The body of those models are eigen-deformations, which are deformations frequently observed in a certain category and span a subspace in a deformation space of the category. For estimating the eigen-deformations, elastic matching and principal component analysis (PCA) were employed. The former was utilized to extract deformations of target patterns automatically. For the online patterns, elastic matching was also utilized to adjust difference in their lengths. The latter was utilized to derive the eigen-deformations as the principal components of the extracted deformations.

The usefulness of the statistical deformation models with eigen-deformations has been confirmed experimentally. The estimated eigen-deformations could represent frequently observed deformations in each character category. In addition, the eigen-deformations were useful for improving accuracy in both of offline and online character recognition tasks.

5. References

Ahmad, T.; Taylor, C. J.; Lanitis, A. & Cootes, T. F. (1997). Tracking and recognising hand gestures, using statistical shape models *Image Vis. Computing*, Vol. 15, pp. 345–352.

Bahlmann, C. & Burkhardt, H.. (2004). The writer independent online handwriting recognition system flog on hand and cluster generative statistical dynamic time warping, *IEEE Trans. PAMI*, Vol. 26, No. 3, pp. 299–310.

Bing, Y.; Ping, C. & Lianfu, J. (2002). Recognizing faces with expressions: within-class space and between-class space, In: *Proc. ICPR*, Vol. 1 of 4, pp. 139–142.

Burr, D. J. (1983). Designing a handwriting reader, *IEEE Trans. PAMI*, Vol. PAMI-5, No. 5, pp. 554–559.

Cho, W.; Lee, S. -W. & Kim, J. H. (1995). Modeling and recognition of cursive words with hidden Markov models, *Pattern Recognit.*, Vol. 28, No. 12, pp. 1941–1953.

Connell, S. D. & Jain,A. K. (2001). Template-based online character recognition, *Pattern Recognit.*, Vol. 34, No. 1, pp. 1–14.

Cootes, T. F.; Taylor, C. J.; Cooper, D. H. & Graham, J. (1995). Active shape models - their training and application, *Comput. Vis. Image Und.*, Vol. 61, No. 1, pp. 38–59.

Deepu, V.; Madhvanath, S. & Ramakrishnan, A. G. (2004). Principal component analysis for online handwritten character recognition, In: *Proc. ICPR*, Vol. 2 of 4 , pp. 327–330.

Fod, A.; Mataric, M. & Jenkins, O. C. (2002). Automated derivation of primitives for movement classification, *Autonomous Robots*, Vol. 12, No. 1, pp. 39–54.

Fujimoto, Y.; Kadota, S.; Hayashi, S.; Yamamoto, M.; Yajima, S. & Yasuda, M. (1976). Recognition of handprinted characters by nonlinear elastic matching, In: *Proc. ICPR*, pp. 113–118.

Guyon, I.; Schomaker, L.; Plamondon, R.; Liberman, M. & Janet, S. (1994). UNIPEN project of on-line data exchange and recognizer benchmarks, In: *Proc. ICPR*, pp. 29–33.

Hase, H.; Shinokawa, T.; Yoneda, M. & Suen, C. Y. (2003). Recognition of rotated characters by eigen-space, In: *Proc. ICDAR*, Vol. 2, pp. 731–735.

Hu, J.; Brown, M. K. & Turin, W. (1996). HMM based on-line handwriting recognition, *IEEE Trans. PAMI*, Vol. 18, No. 10, pp. 1039–1045.

Iwai, Y.; Hata, T. & Yachida, M. (1997). Gesture recognition based on subspace method and hidden Markov model, In: *Proc. IROS*, Vol. 2 of 2, pp. 960–966.

Keysers, D.; Gollan, C. & H. Ney. (2004) . Local context in non-linear deformation models for handwritten character recognition, In: *Proc. ICPR*, Vol. 4, pp. 511–514.

Kimura, F.; Takashina, K. & Tsuruoka, S. (1987). Modified quadratic discriminant functions and the application to Chinese character recognition, *IEEE Trans. PAMI*, Vol. 9, No. 1, pp. 149-153.

Kuo, S. S. & Agazzi, O. E. (1994). Keyword spotting in poorly printed documents using pseudo 2-D hidden Markov models, *IEEE Trans. PAMI*, Vol. 16, No. 8, pp. 842–848.

Lanitis, A.; Taylor, C. J. & Cootes, T. F. (1997). Automatic interpretation and coding of face images using flexible models, *IEEE Trans. PAMI*, Vol. 19, No. 7, pp. 743–756.

Martens, R. & Claesen, L. (1996). On-line signature verification by dynamic time-warping, In: *Proc. ICPR*, pp. 38–42.

Mitoma, H.; Uchida, S. & Sakoe, H. (2005). Online character recognition based on elastic matching and quadratic discrimination, In: *Proc. ICDAR*, Vol. 1 of 2, pp.36–40.

Murase, H. & Nayar, S. K. (1994). Illumination planning for object recognition using parametric eigenspace, *IEEE Trans. PAMI*, Vol. 16, No. 12, pp. 1219–1227.

Nag, R.; Wong,K. H. & F. Fallside. (1986). Script recognition using hidden Markov models, In: *Proc. ICASSP*, Vol. 3, pp. 2071–2074.

Nakai, M.; Akira, N.; Shimodaira, H. & Sagayama S. (2001). Substroke approach to HMM-based on-line Kanji handwriting recognition, In: *Proc. ICDAR*, pp. 491–495.

Naster, C.; Moghaddam, B. & Pentland, A. (1997). Flexible images: matching and recognition using learned deformations, *Comput. Vis. Image Und.*, Vol. 65, No. 2, pp. 179–191.

Oja, E. (1983). *Subspace Methods of Pattern Recognition*, Research Studies Press and J. Wiley.

H. -S. Park & S. -W. Lee. (1998). A truly 2-D hidden Markov model for off-line handwritten character recognition, *Pattern Recognit.*, Vol. 31, No. 12, pp. 1849–1864.

Sanger, T. D. (1995). Optimal movement primitives, *Advances in Neural Info. Proc. Systems*, Vol. 7, pp. 1023–30.

Shen D. & Davatzikos, C. (2000). An adaptive-focus deformable model using statistical and geometric information, *IEEE Trans. PAMI*, Vol. 22, No. 8, pp. 906-913.

Shi, D.; Gunn, S. R. & Damper, R. I. (2003). Handwritten Chinese radical recognition using nonlinear active shape models, *IEEE Trans. PAMI*, Vol. 25, No. 2, pp. 277–280.

Simard, P.; Le Cun, Y.; Denker, J. & Victorri, B. (1992). An efficient algorithm for learning invariances in adaptive classifier, In: *Proc. ICPR*, Vol. 2, pp. 651–655.

Turk, M. & Pentland, A. (1991). "Eigenfaces for recognition," *Journal of Cognitive Neuroscience*, Vol. 3, No. 1, pp. 71–86.

Uchida, S. & Sakoe, H. (2003). Handwritten character recognition using elastic matching based on a class-dependent deformation model, In: *Proc. ICDAR*, Vol. 1 of 2, pp. 163–167.

Uchida, S. & Sakoe, H. (2003). Eigen-deformations for elastic matching based handwritten character recognition, *Pattern Recognit.*, Vol. 36, No. 9, pp. 2031–2040.

Uchida, S. & Sakoe, H. (2005). A survey of elastic matching techniques for handwritten character recognition, *IEICE Trans. Inf. & Syst.*, Vol. E88-D, No. 8, pp. 1781–1790.

Wakahara, T. (1994). Shape matching using LAT and its application to handwritten numeral recognition, *IEEE Trans. PAMI*, Vol. 16, No. 6, pp. 618–629.

Wakahara, T. & Odaka, K. (1997). On-line cursive Kanji character recognition using stroke-based affine transformation, *IEEE Trans. PAMI*, Vol. 19, No. 12, pp. 1381–1385.

Wakahara, T.; Kimura, Y. & A. Tomono. (2001). Affine-invariant recognition of gray-scale characters using global affine transformation correlation, *IEEE Trans. PAMI*, Vol. 23, No. 4, pp. 384–395.

Wang, J.; Wu, C.; Xu, Y.-Q. & Shum, H.-Y. (2005). Combining shape and physical models for online cursive handwriting synthesis, *Int. J. Doc. Ana. Recog.*, Vol. 7, No. 4, pp. 219–227.

Yacoob, Y. & Black, M. (1999). Parameterized modeling and recognition of activities, *Comput. Vis. Image Und.*, Vol. 73, No. 2, pp. 232–247.

Yoshida, K & Sakoe, H. (1982). Online handwritten character recognition for a personal computer system, *IEEE Trans. Consumer Electronics*, Vol. CE-28, No. 3, pp. 202–209.

Zheng, J.; Ding, X.; Wu, Y. & Lu, Z. (1999). Spatio-temporal unified model for on-line handwritten Chinese character recognition, In: *Proc. ICDAR*, pp. 649–652.

2

Character Recognition with Metasets

Bartłomiej Starosta
Polish-Japanese Institute of Information Technology
Poland

1. Introduction

The chapter presents a new approach to the character recognition problem. It is based on metasets – a new concept of sets with partial membership relation. By the character recognition problem we understand determining the similarity degree of the given character sample to the defined character pattern. The discussed mechanism may be applied not only to characters (e.g. letters), but to arbitrary data represented on monochromatic images or even multi-dimensional figures.

The theory of metasets brings a new model of "fuzzy" membership relation for sets. A metaset may be a member of (or equal to) another metaset to variety of different degrees – contrary to classical sets where membership and equality are always either true or false.

The goal of the chapter is to present the application of the new, abstract theory to solving a practical, well-known problem. It develops the method which was partially introduced for some particular case in (Starosta, 2009). The proposed solution had been implemented as a computer program. The experiments made with the program confirm that the theoretical assumptions are correct and the obtained results properly reflect our perception of similarity of characters. It should also be stressed that the concept of metaset itself was partially inspired by another computer application for character recognition, based on neural networks.

1.1 The general idea

The process of determining the similarity degree consists in two stages. Initially, the compound character pattern must be prepared. It consists of several character samples accompanied by quality grades. The samples are depicted on rectangular matrices and they correspond to different forms of the same character. The pattern itself represents various possible approaches to the same character, as a single entity. In the second stage a testing character sample is matched against the pattern and the resulting similarity degree is calculated.

The character samples as well as the compound pattern are encoded as metasets. As the result of matching the testing sample against the pattern we obtain the membership degree of the sample metaset in the pattern metaset and additionally, the sequence of equality degrees of the sample metaset and the pattern elements. The membership degree measures how far the sample resembles the pattern. The equality degrees indicate the similarity of the input sample and each pattern element separately. The membership degrees as well as equality degrees for metasets are expressed as sets of nodes of the binary tree, which are finite binary sequences, and they may be evaluated as real numbers.

The quality grades of the samples in the pattern are membership degrees of the corresponding metasets, too. However, they are manually specified as areas of the matrix for depicting the characters, which contain valid pixels to be included in the matching process. This specification is interpreted as membership degrees of appropriate metasets. The quality grades show how close is a particular sample to the ideal. They may be supplied by experts together with the samples.

The most significant innovation here is treating the membership and equality degrees of metasets as similarity measures for characters provided they are properly encoded as metasets.

1.2 Basic terms and notation

The concept of binary tree plays the key role in the definition of metaset and related notions. Therefore, we start with establishing some well known terms and notation concerning it.

We use the symbol $\mathbb{T}$ for the infinite binary tree with the root $\mathbb{1}$. The nodes of the tree $\mathbb{T}$ are finite binary sequences, the root $\mathbb{1}$ is the empty sequence. For $p \in \mathbb{T}$ the symbol $|p|$ denotes the length of the sequence and $\#p$ denotes the natural number represented by the binary sequence p. Note, that $|\mathbb{1}| = 0$ and we assume $\#\mathbb{1} = 0$. The ordering of nodes in $\mathbb{T}$ is determined by reverse ordering of their lengths: $p \leq q$ whenever $|p| \geq |q|$. In particular the root $\mathbb{1}$ is the largest element in $\mathbb{T}$. The set of nodes of equal length n is called the n-th *level* in the tree: $\mathbb{T}_n = \{\, p \in \mathbb{T} \colon |p| = n \,\}$. The level 0 contains only the root. Nodes of the tree $\mathbb{T}$ are sometimes called *conditions*. If $p \leq q \in \mathbb{T}$, then we say that the condition p is *stronger* than the condition q, and q is *weaker* than p. Thus, the conditions 0 and 1 are stronger than the root $\mathbb{1}$ and they are weaker than the conditions 00, 01, 10, 11, which form the level $\mathbb{T}_2$.

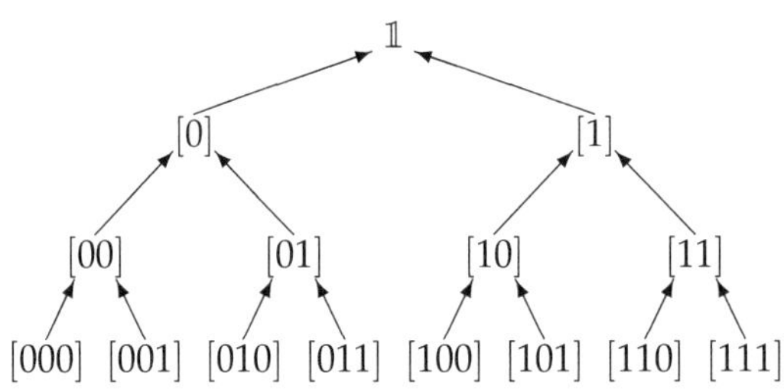

Fig. 1. The binary tree $\mathbb{T}$ and the ordering of nodes (conditions). Arrows point at the larger element, i.e., the weaker condition

A set of nodes $C \subset \mathbb{T}$ is called a *chain* in $\mathbb{T}$, whenever all its elements are pairwise comparable: $\forall_{p,q \in C}\, (p \leq q \vee q \leq p)$. A set $A \subset \mathbb{T}$ is called *antichain* in $\mathbb{T}$, if it consists of mutually incomparable elements: $\forall_{p,q \in A}\, (p \neq q \to \neg\, (p \leq q) \wedge \neg\, (p \geq q))$. On the Fig. 1, the elements $\{\, 00, 01, 100 \,\}$ form a sample antichain. A *maximal antichain* is an antichain which cannot be extended by adding new elements – it is a maximal element with respect to inclusion of antichains. Examples of maximal antichains on the Fig. 1 are $\{\, 0, 1 \,\}$ or $\{\, 00, 01, 1 \,\}$ or even $\{\, \mathbb{1} \,\}$. They are in fact maximal finite antichains (MFA). A *branch* is a maximal chain in the tree $\mathbb{T}$. Note that p is comparable to q only, if there exists a branch containing p and q simultaneously. Similarly, p is incomparable to q, when no branch contains both p and q.

To finish this section we prove a property of maximal finite antichains necessary for evaluating as numbers the degrees represented as sets of nodes. Clearly, there are 2^n nodes on the n-th level of the binary tree, so $\sum_{p \in \mathbb{T}_n} \frac{1}{2^{|p|}} = 1$. This property may be generalized to arbitrary MFA.

Lemma 1. *If $A \subset \mathbb{T}$ is a maximal finite antichain in $\mathbb{T}$, then $\sum_{p \in A} \frac{1}{2^{|p|}} = 1$.*

Proof. Each node $p \neq \mathbb{1}$ is a binary sequence which represents a natural number $\#p$. Therefore, each $p \neq \mathbb{1}$ corresponds to an interval $\bar{p} = [\frac{\#p}{2^{|p|}} \ldots \frac{\#p+1}{2^{|p|}}) \subset [0 \ldots 1]$ and $\mathbb{1}$ corresponds to $I = [0 \ldots 1)$. The length of each interval is $\frac{1}{2^{|p|}}$. For incomparable p and q, the corresponding intervals are disjoint: $\bar{p} \cap \bar{q} = \emptyset$. Indeed, if $\bar{p} \cap \bar{q} \neq \emptyset$, then there must exist some $r \in \mathbb{T}$ such, that $\bar{r} \subset \bar{p} \cap \bar{q}$. Since $\bar{r} \subset \bar{p}$, then $r \leq p$, and similarly $r \leq q$. This implies $p \leq q$ or $q \leq p$, so they are comparable.
We now show, that the measure of $\bigcup_{p \in A} \bar{p}$ is equal 1. Clearly, it cannot be grater than 1, so if it is less, then let $u \subset I \setminus \bigcup_{p \in A} \bar{p}$ be an open interval. There must exist $s \in \mathbb{T}$ such, that $\bar{s} \subset u$. If s is comparable to some $p \in A$, then $\bar{s} \cap \bar{p} \neq \emptyset$, so $\bar{s} \cap \bigcup_{p \in A} \bar{p}$ is non-empty, what contradicts $\bar{s} \subset u$. Thus, assuming that the length of $\bigcup_{p \in A} \bar{p}$ is less than 1 we found s incomparable to all elements of A, what contradicts its maximality.
To complete the proof note, that the length of each $\bar{p}$ is $\frac{1}{2^{|p|}}$, the measure of $\bigcup_{p \in A} \bar{p}$ is 1 and they are all pairwise disjoint. □

2. Metasets

In the classical set theory a set either is an element of another set or it is not; there are no intermediate levels. This binary approach has many vital limitations which make it difficult to apply by representation of vague, imprecise data. Therefore, for the last decades there were several attempts to inventing a concept of set with partial membership relation. Among the most successful ones are fuzzy sets (Zadeh, 1965), intuitionistic fuzzy sets (Atanassov, 1986) and rough sets (Pawlak, 1982). The metaset idea is a new approach to the problem.
One of the most significant characteristics of the metaset concept is its computer oriented design. Definitions of fundamental notions – like membership, equality or algebraic operations – may be formulated in the way which makes them easily implementable using programming languages (Starosta & Kosiński, 2009). This facilitates fast and efficient computer representation and processing of vague data. Additionally, several important theoretical results may be obtained for the metasets which are representable in computers, because of their finite structure. Some of them – like the Lemma 3 – constitute the base for the discussed here mechanism.

2.1 Fundamental concepts

The concept of metaset is strictly based on the classical Zermelo-Fraenkel set theory (ZFC). We define metaset as a set of ordered pairs. The first element of a pair is a member of the metaset, which is another metaset. The second element of the pair is a node of the binary tree which – informally speaking – specifies the membership degree of the first element in the metaset.

Definition 1. A metaset is a crisp set which is either the empty set $\emptyset$ or which has the form:

$$\tau = \{ \langle \sigma, p \rangle : \sigma \text{ is a metaset}, p \in \mathbb{T} \} \ .$$

The definition is recursive, however it is founded by the empty set $\emptyset$, by the Axiom of Foundation in ZFC (Kunen, 1980). First elements of ordered pairs contained in the metaset are called its *potential elements*.

From the classical set theory point of view, a meta set is a relation between a crisp set of other meta sets and a set of nodes of the tree $\mathbb{T}$. Therefore, we adopt some terminology associated with relations. For the given metaset τ the set of its potential elements:

$$\mathrm{dom}(\tau) = \{\, \sigma\colon \langle \sigma, p \rangle \in \tau \,\} \tag{1}$$

is called the *domain* of the metaset τ. Its *range* is the following set:

$$\mathrm{ran}(\tau) = \{\, p\colon \langle \sigma, p \rangle \in \tau \,\} \ . \tag{2}$$

The reader may confirm that $\tau \subset \mathrm{dom}(\tau) \times \mathrm{ran}(\tau) \subset \mathrm{dom}(\tau) \times \mathbb{T}$. For metasets τ and σ the set

$$\tau[\sigma] = \{\, p \in \mathbb{T}\colon \langle \sigma, p \rangle \in \tau \,\} \tag{3}$$

is called the *image* of the metaset τ at the metaset σ. The image $\tau[\sigma]$ is the empty set $\emptyset$, whenever σ is not a potential element of τ.

Example 1. The simplest metaset is the empty set $\emptyset$. It may be a potential element of other metasets:

$$\begin{array}{llll}
\tau = \{\, \langle \emptyset, p \rangle \,\} \ , & \tau[\emptyset] = \{\, p \,\} \ , & \mathrm{dom}(\tau) = \{\, \emptyset \,\} \ , & \mathrm{ran}(\tau) = \{\, p \,\} \ , \\
\sigma = \{\, \langle \emptyset, p \rangle , \langle \emptyset, q \rangle \,\} \ , & \sigma[\emptyset] = \{\, p, q \,\} \ , & \mathrm{dom}(\sigma) = \{\, \emptyset \,\} \ , & \mathrm{ran}(\sigma) = \{\, p, q \,\} \ . \\
\eta = \{\, \langle \tau, p \rangle , \langle \sigma, q \rangle \,\} \ , & \eta[\emptyset] = \emptyset \ , & \mathrm{dom}(\eta) = \{\, \tau, \sigma \,\} \ , & \mathrm{ran}(\eta) = \{\, p, q \,\} \ .
\end{array}$$

Clearly, $\eta[\tau] = p$, $\eta[\sigma] = q$ and since $\emptyset \notin \mathrm{dom}(\eta)$, then $\eta[\emptyset] = \emptyset$.

In this paper we do not deal with metasets in general. We focus here on very specific classes relevant to character recognition problem. Narrowing the domain of discourse simplifies formulations of some results too. We introduce now two classes of metasets used for representation of characters and patterns.
Let A be a maximal finite antichain in $\mathbb{T}$. A non-empty metaset of form

$$\chi \subset \{\, \emptyset \,\} \times A \tag{4}$$

is called *A-sample* metaset. Each non-empty subset $S \subset A$ determines A-sample metaset $\{\, \emptyset \,\} \times S$. A-sample metasets are used for representing character samples.
Let P be a finite set of A-sample metasets. A non-empty metaset of form

$$\pi \subset P \times A \tag{5}$$

is called *A-pattern* metaset. In other words, A-pattern metaset has the form

$$\pi = \bigcup_{i=1}^{i=n} \{\, \chi_i \,\} \times P_i \tag{6}$$

where χ_i are A-sample metasets and $P_i \subset A$, are not empty for $i = 1, \ldots, n$. A-pattern metasets are used for representing character patterns.
We now explain the fundamental technique of interpretation used for defining relations on metasets. Also, it allows to perceive a metaset as a "fuzzy" family of crisp sets. Each member of such family represents some specific, particular point of view on the metaset.

Definition 2. Let τ be a metaset and let $\mathcal{C}$ be a branch in the binary tree $\mathbb{T}$. The interpretation of the metaset τ, given by the branch $\mathcal{C}$, is the following crisp set:

$$\tau_{\mathcal{C}} = \{ \sigma_{\mathcal{C}} \colon \langle \sigma, p \rangle \in \tau \wedge p \in \mathcal{C} \} \ .$$

Thus, branches in $\mathbb{T}$ allow for producing crisp sets out of the metaset. The family of crisp sets $\{ \tau_{\mathcal{C}} \colon \mathcal{C}$ is a branch in $\mathbb{T} \}$ consists of interpretations of the metaset τ. Properties of these interpretations determine properties of the metaset.
Any interpretation of the empty metaset is the empty set itself, independently of the branch: $\emptyset_{\mathcal{C}} = \emptyset$, for each $\mathcal{C} \subset \mathbb{T}$. The process of producing the interpretation of a metaset consists in two stages. In the first stage we remove all the ordered pairs whose second elements are conditions which do not belong to the branch $\mathcal{C}$. The second stage replaces the remaining pairs – whose second elements lie on the branch $\mathcal{C}$ – with interpretations of their first elements, which are other metasets. This two-stage process is repeated recursively on all the levels of the membership hierarchy. As the result we obtain a crisp set.

Example 2. Let $p \in \mathbb{T}$ and let $\tau = \{ \langle \emptyset, p \rangle \}$. If $\mathcal{C}$ is a branch, then

$$\begin{aligned} p \in \mathcal{C} &\rightarrow \tau_{\mathcal{C}} = \{ \emptyset_{\mathcal{C}} \} = \{ \emptyset \} \ , \\ p \notin \mathcal{C} &\rightarrow \tau_{\mathcal{C}} = \emptyset \ . \end{aligned}$$

Depending on the branch the metaset τ acquires different interpretations.

An interpretation of A-sample metaset is either the empty set $\emptyset$ or the singleton $\{ \emptyset \}$. An interpretation of A-pattern metaset $\eta = \{ \langle \sigma, p \rangle \}$, where σ is A-sample metaset, is given by

$$\eta_{\mathcal{C}} = \begin{cases} \emptyset & p \notin \mathcal{C} \ , \\ \{ \emptyset \} & p \in \mathcal{C} \wedge \mathrm{ran}(\sigma) \cap \mathcal{C} = \emptyset \ , \\ \{ \{ \emptyset \} \} & p \in \mathcal{C} \wedge \mathrm{ran}(\sigma) \cap \mathcal{C} \neq \emptyset \ . \end{cases} \tag{7}$$

Therefore, an interpretation of any A-pattern metaset is one of: $\emptyset$, $\{ \emptyset \}$, $\{ \{ \emptyset \} \}$ or $\{ \emptyset, \{ \emptyset \} \}$. For instance, if $\nu = \{ \langle \emptyset, 0 \rangle \}$, $\mu = \{ \langle \emptyset, 111 \rangle \}$, $\tau = \{ \langle \nu, 1 \rangle, \langle \mu, 11 \rangle \}$ and $\mathcal{C} = \{ \mathbb{1}, 1, 11, 111, \ldots \}$ is the rightmost branch, then $\nu_{\mathcal{C}} = \emptyset$, $\mu_{\mathcal{C}} = \{ \emptyset \}$, so $\tau_{\mathcal{C}} = \{ \emptyset, \{ \emptyset \} \}$.
We introduce now basic set-theoretic relations for metasets. All the relations are defined using the same scheme – by referring to interpretations. We start with the membership.

Definition 3. Let τ, σ be metasets and let $p \in \mathbb{T}$. We say that σ belongs to τ under the condition p, if for each branch $\mathcal{C}$ containing p holds $\sigma_{\mathcal{C}} \in \tau_{\mathcal{C}}$. We use the notation $\sigma \epsilon_p \tau$.

Note, that in fact we define an infinite number of membership relations here – each designated with different condition. The membership under the root condition $\sigma \epsilon_{\mathbb{1}} \tau$ corresponds to the crisp, classical membership. The $\mathbb{1}$ designates the highest membership degree, since it is the largest element in $\mathbb{T}$. Stronger conditions designate lower degrees of membership.
We also define an independent set of non-membership relations. The reason for this lies in the fact, that $\neg\, \sigma \epsilon_p \tau$ does not imply that for each branch $\mathcal{C}$ containing p holds $\sigma_{\mathcal{C}} \notin \tau_{\mathcal{C}}$. It merely means that not for each such branch holds $\sigma_{\mathcal{C}} \in \tau_{\mathcal{C}}$, however, there may still exist branches for which it is true.

Definition 4. Let τ, σ be metasets and let $p \in \mathbb{T}$. We say that σ is not a member of τ under the condition p, if for each branch $\mathcal{C}$ containing p holds $\sigma_{\mathcal{C}} \notin \tau_{\mathcal{C}}$. We use the notation $\sigma \not\epsilon_p \tau$.

It might occur strange to the reader that two metasets may be in membership and non-membership relations simultaneously. The relations must be qualified by incomparable conditions, though.

Example 3. Let $\tau = \{ \langle \varnothing, 0 \rangle \}$. We check that $\varnothing \epsilon_0 \tau \ \wedge \ \varnothing \not\epsilon_1 \tau$. Indeed, if $\mathcal{C}^0$ is a branch containing 0, then $\varnothing_{\mathcal{C}^0} = \varnothing \in \{\varnothing\} = \tau_{\mathcal{C}^0}$. Similarly, if $\mathcal{C}^1$ is a branch containing 1, then $\varnothing_{\mathcal{C}^1} = \varnothing \notin \varnothing = \tau_{\mathcal{C}^1}$. Also, $\neg \varnothing \epsilon_{\mathbb{1}} \tau \ \wedge \ \neg \varnothing \not\epsilon_{\mathbb{1}} \tau$, since it is not true, that for each branch $\mathcal{C}$ containing $\mathbb{1}$ holds $\varnothing_{\mathcal{C}} \in \tau_{\mathcal{C}}$ or $\varnothing_{\mathcal{C}} \notin \tau_{\mathcal{C}}$.

As we see, $\neg \sigma \epsilon_p \tau$ does not completely exclude the membership of σ in τ, even for $p = \mathbb{1}$. The fact that $\neg \sigma \epsilon_{\mathbb{1}} \tau$ does not contradict $\sigma \epsilon_p \tau$ for some $p \in \mathbb{T}$. It merely says that σ cannot belong to τ under the condition $\mathbb{1}$. For incomparable conditions p, q it is possible that $\sigma \not\epsilon_p \tau$ and at the same time $\sigma \epsilon_q \tau$. But it is not true that $\sigma \not\epsilon_p \tau \wedge \sigma \epsilon_p \tau$ for any p.
Analogously – by referring to interpretations – we define two sets of equality relations.

Definition 5. Let $p \in \mathbb{T}$ and let τ, σ be metasets. We say that σ is equal to τ under the condition p, if for each branch $\mathcal{C}$ containing p holds $\sigma_{\mathcal{C}} = \tau_{\mathcal{C}}$. We use the notation $\sigma \approx_p \tau$.

Definition 6. Let $p \in \mathbb{T}$ and let τ, σ be metasets. We say that σ is different than τ under the condition p, if for each branch $\mathcal{C}$ containing p holds $\sigma_{\mathcal{C}} \neq \tau_{\mathcal{C}}$. We use the notation $\sigma \not\approx_p \tau$.

Similarly as for conditional membership, it is possible that $\sigma \approx_p \tau \wedge \sigma \not\approx_q \tau$ for some metasets σ, τ and $p, q \in \mathbb{T}$.

Example 4. Let $\tau = \{ \langle \varnothing, \mathbb{1} \rangle \}$ and $\eta = \{ \langle \varnothing, 1 \rangle \}$. For a branch $\mathcal{C}$ containing 0 we have $\tau_{\mathcal{C}} = \{\varnothing\}$ and $\eta_{\mathcal{C}} = \varnothing$. On the other hand, if $\mathcal{C}$ contains 1, then we have $\tau_{\mathcal{C}} = \{\varnothing\} = \eta_{\mathcal{C}}$. Thus, $\tau \not\approx_0 \eta$ and $\tau \approx_1 \eta$. However, $\neg \tau \approx_{\mathbb{1}} \eta \wedge \neg \tau \not\approx_{\mathbb{1}} \eta$.

The following lemma is the metaset version of the obvious fact known from the crisp set theory: $x = y \wedge y \in z \to x \in z$.

Lemma 2. *If $p \in \mathbb{T}$ and τ, σ, λ are metasets such, that $\tau \approx_p \sigma$ and $\sigma \epsilon_p \lambda$, then also $\tau \epsilon_p \lambda$.*

Proof. If $\mathcal{C}$ is an arbitrary branch containing p, then by the assumptions $\tau_{\mathcal{C}} = \sigma_{\mathcal{C}}$ and $\sigma_{\mathcal{C}} \in \lambda_{\mathcal{C}}$. Therefore, also $\tau_{\mathcal{C}} \in \lambda_{\mathcal{C}}$, what implies $\tau \epsilon_p \lambda$. □

The certainty grades for relations on metasets are represented by sets of nodes of the binary tree and they may be evaluated as real numbers. We do not develop the general theory here, the interested reader is referred to (Starosta, 2010). Instead, we show how to evaluate the degrees of membership, non-membership, equality and difference for A-sample metasets and A-pattern metasets, when the maximal finite antichain A is fixed. Let σ, η be A-sample metasets and let τ be A-pattern metaset. The following sets contained in A

$$\mathrm{M}(\sigma, \tau) = \{ p \in A \colon \sigma \epsilon_p \tau \} \ , \tag{8}$$
$$\mathrm{N}(\sigma, \tau) = \{ p \in A \colon \sigma \not\epsilon_p \tau \} \ , \tag{9}$$
$$\mathrm{E}(\sigma, \eta) = \{ p \in A \colon \sigma \approx_p \eta \} \ , \tag{10}$$
$$\mathrm{D}(\sigma, \eta) = \{ p \in A \colon \sigma \not\approx_p \eta \} \ , \tag{11}$$

are called *membership, non-membership, equality* and *difference sets* for σ and τ (or η) respectively. The values

$$\mathrm{m}(\sigma,\tau) = \sum_{p \in \mathrm{M}(\sigma,\tau)} \frac{1}{2^{|p|}} , \tag{12}$$

$$\mathrm{n}(\sigma,\tau) = \sum_{p \in \mathrm{N}(\sigma,\tau)} \frac{1}{2^{|p|}} , \tag{13}$$

$$\mathrm{e}(\sigma,\eta) = \sum_{p \in \mathrm{E}(\sigma,\eta)} \frac{1}{2^{|p|}} , \tag{14}$$

$$\mathrm{d}(\sigma,\eta) = \sum_{p \in \mathrm{D}(\sigma,\eta)} \frac{1}{2^{|p|}} , \tag{15}$$

are called the *membership, non-membership, equality* and *difference values* of σ in τ (or η) respectively. Clearly, by the Lemma 1 all they range between 0 and 1, inclusive.
It is worth stressing, that A-sample metasets and A-pattern metasets have the following important property.

Lemma 3. *Let A be a maximal finite antichain. Let σ, η be arbitrary A-sample metasets and let τ be arbitrary A-pattern metaset. The following equations hold:*

$$\mathrm{m}(\sigma,\tau) + \mathrm{n}(\sigma,\tau) = 1 , \tag{16}$$

$$\mathrm{e}(\sigma,\eta) + \mathrm{d}(\sigma,\eta) = 1 . \tag{17}$$

Proof. First, observe that $\mathrm{M}(\sigma,\tau) \cap \mathrm{N}(\sigma,\tau) = \emptyset$ and $\mathrm{E}(\sigma,\eta) \cap \mathrm{D}(\sigma,\eta) = \emptyset$. Indeed, it is not possible that for some $p \in A$ simultaneously hold $\sigma \,\epsilon_p\, \tau$ and $\sigma \not\epsilon_p\, \tau$ or $\sigma \approx_p \eta$ and $\sigma \not\approx_p \eta$. Therefore, by using the Lemma 1 we may reformulate the thesis as follows:

$$\mathrm{M}(\sigma,\tau) \cup \mathrm{N}(\sigma,\tau) = A , \tag{18}$$

$$\mathrm{E}(\sigma,\eta) \cup \mathrm{D}(\sigma,\eta) = A . \tag{19}$$

To prove (18) it is enough to show, that for each $p \in A$ either $\sigma \,\epsilon_p\, \tau$ or $\sigma \not\epsilon_p\, \tau$ is true. In other words, either for all branches $\mathcal{C}$ containing p holds $\sigma_{\mathcal{C}} \in \tau_{\mathcal{C}}$ or for all such branches holds $\sigma_{\mathcal{C}} \notin \tau_{\mathcal{C}}$. Clearly, for any branch $\mathcal{C}$ either $\sigma_{\mathcal{C}}$ is a member of $\tau_{\mathcal{C}}$ or not, the question is whether the (non-)membership is maintained for all interpretations determined by a $p \in A$. This is true for A-sample metaset σ and A-pattern metaset τ, since $\mathrm{ran}(\sigma) \subset A$ and $\mathrm{ran}(\tau) \subset A$ and also $\bigcup_{\eta \in \mathrm{dom}(\tau)} \mathrm{ran}(\eta) \subset A$. Therefore, there exist no conditions stronger than p which could affect the interpretations. In other words, if $\mathcal{C}'$ and $\mathcal{C}''$ are different branches containing $p \in A$, then $\tau_{\mathcal{C}'} = \tau_{\mathcal{C}''}$ and $\sigma_{\mathcal{C}'} = \sigma_{\mathcal{C}''}$. The proof of (19) is analogous. □

The lemma says that there is no hesitancy in membership or equality for such metasets. This is not true for metasets in general. There exist metasets α, β with infinite ranges such, that for any $p \in \mathbb{T}$ neither $\alpha \,\epsilon_p\, \beta$ nor $\alpha \not\epsilon_p\, \beta$ is true, see (Starosta, 2010) for details. When we translate this property into the language of character recognition, then it says that for each pixel of a character we may decide whether it matches some pattern (or another character) or not. There is not any doubt about it.

2.2 Properties relevant to character recognition

In this section we prove some technical facts strictly relevant to character recognition mechanism. We refer to them in the sequel. Proofs are not required for understanding the idea so they may be skipped on first reading. We supply them for mathematical completeness and clarity.

The following lemma tells that for two given A-sample metasets τ and σ, their conditional difference is determined by the elements of the symmetric difference of their ranges: $\operatorname{ran}(\tau) \vartriangle \operatorname{ran}(\sigma)$, whereas their conditional equality is determined by the complement to A of the symmetric difference: $A \setminus (\operatorname{ran}(\tau) \vartriangle \operatorname{ran}(\sigma))$.

We may express this property in terms of character recognition as follows. When comparing two characters, then not only the pixels belonging to them simultaneously affect the result of comparison, but also the pixels that belong to background of both. If a pixel belongs to one of the characters and for another character the same pixel forms the background, then such pixel asserts the difference between the characters.

Lemma 4. *Let A be a finite maximal antichain in $\mathbb{T}$ and let $S, T \subset A$ be not empty. Let $\tau = \{\emptyset\} \times T$ and $\sigma = \{\emptyset\} \times S$. For $R = S \cap T \cup (A \setminus S) \cap (A \setminus T)$ the following implications hold:*

$$r \in R \;\rightarrow\; \tau \approx_r \sigma \;, \tag{20}$$

$$r \in A \setminus R \;\rightarrow\; \tau \not\approx_r \sigma \;. \tag{21}$$

Proof. Assume that $r \in S \cap T$. If C is a branch containing r, then clearly $\tau_C = \{\emptyset\} = \sigma_C$, and therefore $\tau \approx_r \sigma$. If $r \in (A \setminus S) \cap (A \setminus T)$ and C is a branch containing r, then $\tau_C = \emptyset = \sigma_C$, so $\tau \approx_r \sigma$ holds too. This proves (20).

To prove (21) note, that:

$$\begin{aligned} A \setminus R &= A \setminus (T \cap S \cup (A \setminus T) \cap (A \setminus S)) \;, \\ &= (A \setminus T \cap S) \cap (A \setminus (A \setminus T) \cap (A \setminus S)) \;, \\ &= (A \setminus T \cap S) \cap (T \cup S) \;, \\ &= ((A \setminus T) \cup (A \setminus S)) \cap (T \cup S) \;, \\ &= (A \setminus T) \cap S \cup (A \setminus S) \cap T \;, \\ &= (S \setminus T) \cup (T \setminus S) \;, \\ &= S \vartriangle T \;. \end{aligned}$$

If $r \in (A \setminus T) \cap S$, and C is a branch containing r, then $\tau_C = \emptyset$ and $\sigma_C = \{\emptyset\}$, so $\tau \not\approx_r \sigma$. Similarly, if $r \in (A \setminus S) \cap T$, then $\tau_C = \{\emptyset\}$ and $\sigma_C = \emptyset$, so $\tau \not\approx_r \sigma$. Thus, for $r \in A \setminus R$ we obtain $\tau \not\approx_r \sigma$. □

The set R is the equality set for τ and σ, and $A \setminus R$ is the difference set:

$$R = \mathrm{E}(\tau, \sigma) \;, \tag{22}$$

$$A \setminus R = \mathrm{D}(\tau, \sigma) \;. \tag{23}$$

The Lemma 4 enables evaluation of the equality degree of metasets representing character samples, i.e., the similarity of two characters.

We now prove the main result which shows the construction of the membership and non-membership sets for the given A-sample metaset and A-pattern metaset. In other words,

it allows for evaluation of the similarity degree of a character testing sample (CTS) to the compound character pattern (CCP).
In the following theorem the metaset σ represents the testing sample (CTS), ρ is the compound character pattern (CCP) built up of potential elements π^i representing characters. The sets P^i and S constitute the structures of the pattern samples and the input sample. The sets Q^i represent equality degrees of the CTS and CCP elements ans the sets R^i represent the qualities of CCP members.

Theorem 5. *Let A be a maximal finite antichain in $\mathbb{T}$ and let $i = 1, \ldots, k$. Let $P^i, R^i, S \subset A$ be not empty. Let $\sigma = \{\emptyset\} \times S$, $\pi^i = \{\emptyset\} \times P^i$ and $\rho = \bigcup_{i=1}^{k} \left\{ \pi^i \right\} \times R^i$ be metasets. For the sets $Q^i = S \cap P^i \cup (A \setminus S) \cap (A \setminus P^i)$ and $U = \bigcup_{i=1}^{k} Q^i \cap R^i$, the following holds:*

$$q \in Q^i \rightarrow \sigma \approx_q \pi^i \ , \tag{24}$$
$$q \in A \setminus Q^i \rightarrow \sigma \not\approx_q \pi^i \ , \tag{25}$$
$$u \in U \rightarrow \sigma \epsilon_u \rho \ , \tag{26}$$
$$u \in A \setminus U \rightarrow \sigma \not\epsilon_u \rho \ . \tag{27}$$

Proof. The Lemma 4 proves (24) and (25).
To prove (26) take $u \in U$. There exists $i \in \{1 \ldots k\}$ such, that $u \in R^i \cap Q^i$. By (24) this implies $\sigma \approx_u \pi^i$, since $u \in Q^i$. By the construction of ρ – $u \in R^i$, so $\left\langle \pi^i, u \right\rangle \in \rho$ – and by the Definition 3 we have $\pi^i \epsilon_u \rho$. Thus, by the Lemma 2 we obtain $\sigma \epsilon_u \rho$.
To prove (27) let $R = \bigcup_{i=1}^{k} R^i$ and let $\bar{Q}^i = A \setminus Q^i$. We may split each R^i into two parts: $R^i = \left(R^i \setminus Q^i\right) \cup \left(R^i \cap Q^i\right) = R^i \cap \bar{Q}^i \cup R^i \cap Q^i$. Therefore,

$$R = \bigcup_{i=1}^{k} R^i \cap \bar{Q}^i \cup \bigcup_{i=1}^{k} R^i \cap Q^i = \bigcup_{i=1}^{k} \left(R^i \cap \bar{Q}^i\right) \cup U \ . \tag{28}$$

Let $u \in A \setminus U$ and let $\mathcal{C}$ be a branch containing u. Note, that $U \subset R \subset A$, so we consider two cases: $u \in R \setminus U$ and $u \in A \setminus R$.
If $u \in R \setminus U$, then let $I \subset \{1 \ldots k\}$ be the set of all those i, for which $u \in R^i \cap \bar{Q}^i$. Since $u \in \mathcal{C}$ and for each $i \in I$ the intersection $R^i \cap \mathcal{C}$ contains at most one element (which is u), then by the Definition 2

$$\rho_{\mathcal{C}} = \left\{ \pi^i_{\mathcal{C}} \colon 1 \leq i \leq k \wedge R^i \cap \mathcal{C} \neq \emptyset \right\} = \left\{ \pi^i_{\mathcal{C}} \colon 1 \leq i \leq k \wedge u \in R^i \right\} = \left\{ \pi^i_{\mathcal{C}} \colon i \in I \right\} \ . \tag{29}$$

The last equality is implied by the following (since $u \notin U$):

$$\left\{ i \colon u \in R^i \right\} = \left\{ i \colon u \in R^i \cap \bar{Q}^i \right\} \cup \left\{ i \colon u \in R^i \cap Q^i \right\} = I \cup \emptyset = I \ . \tag{30}$$

Thus, for $i \in I$ we have $\pi^i_{\mathcal{C}} \in \rho_{\mathcal{C}}$. However, for $i \in I$ we also have $u \notin Q^i$, so by (25) holds $\sigma \not\approx_u \pi^i$ and consequently $\sigma_{\mathcal{C}} \neq \pi^i_{\mathcal{C}}$. Since $\sigma_{\mathcal{C}}$ is different than all the members of $\rho_{\mathcal{C}}$, then $\sigma_{\mathcal{C}} \notin \rho_{\mathcal{C}}$ for any branch $\mathcal{C} \ni u$, what gives $\sigma \not\epsilon_u \rho$. This proves (27) for the case when $u \in R \setminus U$.
If $u \in A \setminus R$, then for $\mathcal{C} \ni u$ we have $\rho_{\mathcal{C}} = \emptyset$, so $\sigma \not\epsilon_u \rho$ for any σ, what implies the second case for (27). □

The set U is the membership set for σ in ρ, and $A \setminus U$ is the non-membership set:

$$U = \mathrm{M}(\sigma,\rho) \ , \tag{31}$$

$$A \setminus U = \mathrm{N}(\sigma,\rho) \ . \tag{32}$$

The sequence of equality sets $Q^i = \mathrm{E}(\sigma,\pi^i)$ enables evaluation of equality degrees of A-sample metaset σ and potential elements π^i of A-pattern metaset ρ. They show the distribution of the overall similarity degree among the pattern elements.

3. Character recognition with metasets

In this section we explain the core of the idea of applying metasets to recognition of characters. We show how to represent characters and compound character patterns as metasets. Then we we show how to calculate appropriate membership and equality degrees and interpret them as quality grades of the input samples.

The procedure we discuss here involves two stages. During the first stage we define the compound character pattern (CCP). It represents a single character and it is comprised of a number of different samples of the character. The samples are graded with quality grades.

In the second stage we supply character testing samples (CTS) and we calculate the result which is the similarity degree of CTS to CCP. The similarity degree tells how close is the CTS to the character represented by CCP. Besides the overall similarity degree we obtain also the sequence of similarity degrees of the CTS to each member of the CCP. These degrees show how close is the input sample to each element of the compound pattern.

The compound character pattern is represented by a metaset, whose potential elements represent particular character samples of the pattern. The testing sample is represented by a metaset too. The resulting similarity degree is the membership degree of CTS in CCP. The additional similarity degrees of CTS to pattern elements are partial equality degrees of CTS to potential elements of CCP.

One of the goals of this section is to convince the reader that partial membership and equality degrees of metasets encoding character samples properly reflect the human perception of similarity of characters.

3.1 Representing characters as metasets

Characters are displayed on the matrix X_r^c comprised of r rows and c columns (shortly: X). The natural numbers r and c may be arbitrary, however they must remain constant throughout the matching process: all the character samples in the CCP pattern as well as all the CTS input samples must use the same matrix dimensions. We focus on monochromatic images here, so the cells of the matrix acquire two states: selected ones belong to the character and deselected ones form the background. For the given character a displayed on the matrix, the set of selected cells is denoted by Xa.

Prior to defining character samples, a mapping $m\colon X \mapsto \mathbb{T}$ between matrix cells and nodes of the binary tree must be established. To each cell of the matrix a node of the binary tree must be assigned so that the set of assigned nodes – denoted by $m(X)$ – forms a maximal antichain A in the tree $\mathbb{T}$. The assignment of nodes to cells is arbitrary – no special ordering is required. The antichain and the mapping are constant for the whole character matching process – all the CTS and CCP samples use the same A and m. Note, that since the nodes assigned to cells form a MFA, then any branch in the tree contains exactly one assigned node.

The simplest example of such assignment is when $r \cdot c = 2^k$ for some k. In such case the nodes of the k-th level of the binary tree may be assigned in an arbitrary way to the cells. We call such one-to-one mapping of matrix and some level in $\mathbb{T}$ an *even* mapping. The Figure 2 demonstrates a sample 4×4 matrix with a mapping $m\colon X_4^4 \mapsto \mathbb{T}_4$ onto the level 4 of the tree. For simplicity, most examples will be based on this 4×4 matrix and the mapping.

0000	0001	0010	0011
0100	0101	0110	0111
1000	1001	1010	1011
1100	1101	1110	1111

Fig. 2. A standard mapping of the level 4 of the binary tree $\mathbb{T}$ to cells of the 4×4 matrix.

When $r \cdot c \neq 2^k$ for any $k \in \mathbb{N}$, then the cells of the matrix must be mapped to nodes from different levels of $\mathbb{T}$, since levels contain 2^k nodes. Anyway, the image $m(X_r^c)$ must be a MFA. We call such a mapping *uneven*. See Fig. 3 for an example of uneven 3×4 mapping.

11100	000	001	11110
1100	010	011	1101
11101	100	101	11111

Fig. 3. Mapping of some antichain in $\mathbb{T}$ to cells of the 3×4 matrix.

For an even mapping the placement of particular nodes is rather irrelevant. On the other hand, when the mapping is uneven, then the nodes from different levels assigned to cells impose the following interpretation. Parts of the matrix which are more important for the particular character, and which we want to stress somehow by distinguishing it from the rest, are associated with nodes which are closer to the root – the weaker conditions. The cells which are of less importance contain nodes from lower levels of the tree – the stronger conditions. Weaker conditions have more impact on the resulting membership and equality degrees than stronger ones (cf. Equations 12–15). For instance we might be particularly interested in proper recognizing of the dot over the letter 'i'. In such case we may use the assignment depicted on the Fig. 4. The reader is encouraged to check that the nodes form a maximal antichain. The cells containing the nodes 10 and 110 are more sensitive to errors than other cells and they influence the resulting similarity degree more than others.

0000	10	0100
0001	110	0101
0010	1110	0110
0011	1111	0111

Fig. 4. Simple assignment for stressing the dot over 'i'.

Note, that even when $r \cdot c = 2^k$ for some k, then the mapping might be uneven too, since we may assign nodes from different levels to cells in order to stress some areas of the matrix and diminish the influence of others. Anyway, the requirement that the range forms a maximal antichain must be fulfilled. The assignment on the Fig. 5 shows how to stress the upper-left corner of the X_2^2 matrix. The impact of the lower row is much less than the impact of the upper row in this case.

0	10
110	111

Fig. 5. Uneven assignment for 2×2 matrix.

We now construct the metaset χ representing the character denoted by a displayed on the matrix X. The domain of the metaset consists of the empty set only: $\mathrm{dom}(\chi) = \{\emptyset\}$. The set $m(Xa) \subset A$ of nodes corresponding to the marked cells of the matrix forms the range of the metaset representing the sample: $\mathrm{ran}(\chi) = m(Xa)$. Since the domain of χ contains exactly one element $\emptyset$, then $\mathrm{ran}(\chi) = \chi[\emptyset]$. Thus,

$$\chi = \{\emptyset\} \times m(Xa) \ . \tag{33}$$

Note, that we interpret the membership degree of $\emptyset$ in χ as the set of selected cells of the character. This membership degree is irrelevant by itself, however, it determines the equality degree of this sample and any other CTS supplied during the recognition phase. It also affects the overall result which is the membership degree of the CTS in the CCP.
As an example, let us represent the character 'c' on the 4×4 matrix with the standard assignment, like on the Fig. 6. The metaset representing this letter is

$$\begin{aligned} \chi = \{ \ & \langle\emptyset,0001\rangle, \langle\emptyset,0010\rangle, \langle\emptyset,0011\rangle, \langle\emptyset,0100\rangle, \\ & \langle\emptyset,1000\rangle, \langle\emptyset,1101\rangle, \langle\emptyset,1110\rangle, \langle\emptyset,1111\rangle \ \} \ . \end{aligned} \tag{34}$$

The set of nodes corresponding to the selected cells is

$$m(X\mathtt{c}) = \{ 0001, 0010, 0011, 0100, 1000, 1101, 1110, 1111 \} \ . \tag{35}$$

	0001	0010	0011
0100			
1000			
	1101	1110	1111

Fig. 6. The character 'c' represented on the 4×4 matrix.

3.2 Defining the compound pattern

Defining the compound character pattern (CCP) is the essential step in the process of character recognition with metasets. The CCP consists of a number of character samples accompanied by quality grades. The samples describe some point of view on the character. The different shapes collected together give an idea of how the character should look like. They may be supplied by independent experts or they may be samples of hand-writing retrieved from different persons.

The most important factor here is defining the quality grades for samples included in the CCP as sets of nodes of the binary tree. Instead of giving them numerical values – as it is usually done – initially we define quality grades to be the parts of the character matrix which contain valid data, for each sample separately. Thus, the quality grade of a character sample is the set of cells containing correct, necessary pixels of the character or its background. For each sample, the cells of the matrix which are considered bad, missing or not important are excluded by the quality grade area and therefore, they are not taken into account during the recognition process. The mapping m transforms this quality set into a subset of the maximal finite antichain A, which may be evaluated as a number then, however some part of information is lost this way (i.e., which exactly cells are taken into account and which are considered invalid).

Associating character samples represented as A-sample metasets with the corresponding quality grades represented as subsets of A we create the A-pattern metaset representing the CCP. Then, testing character samples represented by other A-sample metasets are matched against the A-pattern metaset.

If we denote characters included in the CCP with the variables $c_1, c_2, \ldots$, then $Xc_1, Xc_2, \ldots$ are the sets of cells of the matrix which contain their pixels – the selected cells. The metasets corresponding to the characters are denoted with $\chi_1, \chi_2, \ldots$ (cf. Equation 33):

$$\chi_i = \{\emptyset\} \times m(Xc_i) \ . \tag{36}$$

The corresponding quality grades $q_1, q_2, \ldots$, when expressed as sets of cells of the matrix X are denoted with $Xq_1, Xq_2, \ldots$. Thus, $m(Xq_1), m(Xq_2), \ldots$ are subsets of A specifying quality grades of characters $c_1, c_2, \ldots$, or – in other words – they are membership degrees of the A-sample metasets χ_i in the A-pattern metaset π representing the CCP, which is defined as follows (n is the number of samples in the pattern):

$$\pi = \bigcup_{i=1}^{i=n} \{\chi_i\} \times m(Xq_i) \ . \tag{37}$$

The complete structure of the A-pattern metaset π representing the compound character pattern comprised of the characters $c_1, \ldots, c_n$ accompanied by the quality grades $q_1, \ldots, q_n$ is depicted by the following equation

$$\pi = \bigcup_{i=1}^{i=n} \{\, \{\emptyset\} \times m(Xc_i) \,\} \times m(Xq_i). \tag{38}$$

We illustrate the above formulas with an example. We use the X_4^4 matrix with the standard mapping m onto the antichain $A = \mathbb{T}_4$ which is the 4th level of the tree (cf. Fig.2). The Figure 7 depicts three different samples of the letter 'c'. Pixels of characters are those containing binary sequences. Invalid cells are marked gray; the cells without background form the quality grades.

We understand that the areas of the matrix with gray background contain pixels which are either unreadable or we are not sure whether they are selected or not, or they are distorted

	0001	0010	
0100			
1000			
	1101	1110	

0000	0001	0010	
0100			
1000			
1100	1101	1110	

	0001	0010	0011
0100	0101		
1000	1001		
	1101	1110	1111

Fig. 7. Three samples c_1, c_2, c_3 of letter 'c'. Cells without gray background make up quality grades.

somehow, and therefore they cannot be included in the representation of the character without causing any doubt. They may also be treated as a mask for excluding parts of the matrix from the matching process. Anyway, when calculating equality degrees the whole matrix area is taken into account, so excluded parts play role in determining the membership (similarity) degree to the CCP only.
The sets of nodes corresponding to the selected cells of the characters c_1, c_2 and c_3 on the Fig. 7 are shown by the following equations:

$$m(Xc_1) = \{\, 0001, 0010, 0100, 1000, 1101, 1110 \,\} \ , \tag{39}$$
$$m(Xc_2) = \{\, 0000, 0001, 0010, 0100, 1000, 1100, 1101, 1110 \,\} \ , \tag{40}$$
$$m(Xc_3) = \{\, 0001, 0010, 0011, 0100, 0101, 1000, 1001, 1101, 1110, 1111 \,\} \ . \tag{41}$$

The A-sample metasets χ_1, χ_2, χ_3 representing these characters have form (cf. Equation 36):

$$\chi_1 = \{\ \langle\varnothing, 0001\rangle, \langle\varnothing, 0010\rangle, \langle\varnothing, 0100\rangle, \langle\varnothing, 1000\rangle, \langle\varnothing, 1101\rangle, \langle\varnothing, 1110\rangle\ \} \ , \tag{42}$$
$$\chi_2 = \{\ \langle\varnothing, 0000\rangle, \langle\varnothing, 0001\rangle, \langle\varnothing, 0010\rangle, \langle\varnothing, 0100\rangle, \langle\varnothing, 1000\rangle, \langle\varnothing, 1100\rangle, \langle\varnothing, 1101\rangle, \langle\varnothing, 1110\rangle\ \} \ , \tag{43}$$
$$\chi_3 = \{\ \langle\varnothing, 0001\rangle, \langle\varnothing, 0010\rangle, \langle\varnothing, 0011\rangle, \langle\varnothing, 0100\rangle, \langle\varnothing, 0101\rangle, \langle\varnothing, 1000\rangle, \langle\varnothing, 1101\rangle, \langle\varnothing, 1101\rangle, \langle\varnothing, 1110\rangle, \langle\varnothing, 1111\rangle\ \} \ . \tag{44}$$

They comprise the domain of the A-pattern metaset π: $\mathrm{dom}(\pi) = \{\, \chi_1, \chi_2, \chi_3 \,\}$. The quality grades q_i of the samples c_i – represented by the cells without gray background – when mapped to subsets of A with the mapping m, make up the membership degrees $m(Xq_i)$ of χ_i in the π:

$$\pi[\chi_i] = m(Xq_i), \ \text{for } i = 1, 2, 3 \ . \tag{45}$$

From the Fig. 7 we may read that

$$m(Xq_1) = \{\, 0000, 0001, 0010, 0011, 0100, 0101, 0110, 1000, 1001, 1100 \,\} = \mathbb{T}_4 \setminus \{\, 0111, 1010, 1011, 1101, 1110, 1111 \,\} \ , \tag{46}$$
$$m(Xq_2) = \{\, 0100, 0101, 1000, 1001, 1010, 1100, 1101, 1110 \,\} = \mathbb{T}_4 \setminus \{\, 0000, 0001, 0010, 0011, 0110, 0111, 1011, 1111 \,\} \ , \tag{47}$$
$$m(Xq_3) = \{\, 0011, 0110, 0111, 1010, 1011, 1111 \,\} = \mathbb{T}_4 \setminus \{\, 0000, 0001, 0010, 0100, 0101, 1000, 1001, 1100, 1101, 1110 \,\} \ . \tag{48}$$

Thus, the A-pattern metaset π representing the CCP has the following complete structure:

$$\begin{aligned}\pi &= \{\chi_1\} \times m(Xq_1) \cup \{\chi_2\} \times m(Xq_2) \cup \{\chi_3\} \times m(Xq_3) \\ &= \{\{\emptyset\} \times \{0001, 0010, 0100, 1000, 1101, 1110\}\} \\ &\quad \times \{0000, 0001, 0010, 0011, 0100, 0101, 0110, 1000, 1001, 1100\} \\ &\cup \{\{\emptyset\} \times \{0000, 0001, 0010, 0100, 1000, 1100, 1101, 1110\}\} \\ &\quad \times \{0100, 0101, 1000, 1001, 1010, 1100, 1101, 1110\} \\ &\cup \{\{\emptyset\} \times \{0001, 0010, 0011, 0100, 0101, 1000, 1001, 1101, 1110, 1111\}\} \\ &\quad \times \{0011, 0110, 0111, 1010, 1011, 1111\} \ . \end{aligned} \tag{49}$$

For each $\chi_i \in \mathrm{dom}(\pi)$ the numerical values of the membership degrees of χ_i in π, equal to their numerical quality grades, are given by the formula (cf. Equation 12):

$$\mathrm{m}(\chi_i, \pi) = \sum_{p \in \pi[\chi_i]} \frac{1}{2^{|p|}} \ , \tag{50}$$

and they are equal 0.62, 0.5 and 0.38, for the characters c_1, c_2, c_3 respectively (the reader is encouraged to verify it). The numerical representation of the degree looses information concerning the particular cells taken into account. For instance, there are many combinations of cells for which the above formula gives the result of 0.5. The numerical value is more human-friendly, however.

3.3 Evaluating similarity degrees

Once the compound character pattern (CCP) is prepared we are ready to supply testing character samples (CTS) and evaluate their similarity degrees. The CTS is represented as a metaset in exactly the same manner as CCP elements, i.e., we use the same matrix X with the same mapping m of cells to some maximal finite antichain A.

The process of matching the input character sample represented by the A-sample metaset τ against the prepared compound character pattern represented by the A-pattern metaset π involves calculation of the membership degree of τ in π and the sequence of equality degrees of τ and potential elements χ_i of π. The membership degree tells us to what measure the CTS resembles the character defined by the CCP and is represented by the set $\mathrm{M}(\tau, \pi)$ (see Equation 8). The equality degrees play supplemental role and they show the similarity of τ and each pattern element separately, which – contrary to the CCP – are single characters. They are represented by the sets $\mathrm{E}(\tau, \chi_i)$ (see Equation 10). We apply here the Theorem 5 for determining the similarity degrees and also the Equations 12–15 for numerical evaluation of the degres.

Let us make calculations for the sample letter 'c' shown on the Fig. 6. The metaset χ representing the character is defined by the Equation (34). First, we establish the notation. The left hand sides of the following equations correspond to variables used in the Theorem 5 and in the right hand sides we use metasets defined in previous sections, $i = 1, 2, 3$.

$$\sigma = \chi \qquad \text{the CTS, see Fig. 6 and Equation 34} \ , \tag{51}$$

$$\pi^i = \chi_i \qquad \text{the pattern elements, see Equations 42–44} \ , \tag{52}$$

$$\rho = \pi \qquad \text{the CCP, see Fig. 7 and Equation 49} \ , \tag{53}$$

$$S = m(X\mathtt{c}) \qquad \text{the CTS selected cells, see Equation 35} \ , \tag{54}$$

$$P^i = m(Xc_i) \quad \text{the selected cells of CCP elements, see Fig. 7 and Equations 39–41} \;, \tag{55}$$

$$R^i = m(Xq_i) \quad \text{the CCP quality marks, see Equations 46–48} \;, \tag{56}$$

$$Q^i = \mathrm{E}(\chi, \chi_i) \quad \text{the equality sets, see Equations 10 and 22–23} \;, \tag{57}$$

$$U = \mathrm{M}(\chi, \pi) \quad \text{the membership set, see Equations 8 and 31–32} \;. \tag{58}$$

We start with calculating the sets Q^i, Recall, that the antichain A is equal to the level $\mathbb{T}_4$ of the tree and the mapping m is shown of the Fig. 2.

$$\begin{aligned}
\mathrm{E}(\chi_1, \chi) = Q^1 &= S \cap P^1 \cup (A \setminus S) \cap (A \setminus P^1) \\
&= \{\,0001, 0010, 0011, 0100, 1000, 1101, 1110, 1111\,\} \\
&\quad \cap \{\,0001, 0010, 0100, 1000, 1101, 1110\,\} \\
&\quad \cup \{\,0000, 0101, 0110, 0111, 1001, 1010, 1011, 1100\,\} \\
&\quad \cap \{\,0000, 0011, 0101, 0110, 0111, 1001, 1010, 1011, 1100, 1111\,\} \\
&= P^1 \cup (A \setminus S) \\
&= \{\,0001, 0010, 0100, 1000, 1101, 1110\,\} \\
&\quad \cup \{\,0000, 0101, 0110, 0111, 1001, 1010, 1011\,\} \\
&= \mathbb{T}_4 \setminus \{\,0011, 1111\,\} \;.
\end{aligned}$$

$$\begin{aligned}
\mathrm{E}(\chi_2, \chi) = Q^2 &= S \cap P^2 \cup (A \setminus S) \cap (A \setminus P^2) \\
&= \{\,0001, 0010, 0011, 0100, 1000, 1101, 1110, 1111\,\} \\
&\quad \cap \{\,0000, 0001, 0010, 0100, 1000, 1100, 1101, 1110\,\} \\
&\quad \cup \{\,0000, 0101, 0110, 0111, 1001, 1010, 1011, 1100\,\} \\
&\quad \cap \{\,0011, 0101, 0110, 0111, 1001, 1010, 1011, 1111\,\} \\
&= P^2 \setminus \{\,0000, 1100\,\} \;\cup\; (A \setminus S) \setminus \{\,0000, 1100\,\} \\
&= \{\,0001, 0010, 0100, 1000, 1101, 1110\,\} \\
&\quad \cup \{\,0101, 0110, 0111, 1001, 1010, 1011\,\} \\
&= \mathbb{T}_4 \setminus \{\,0000, 0011, 1100, 1111\,\} \;.
\end{aligned}$$

$$\begin{aligned}
\mathrm{E}(\chi_3, \chi) = Q^3 &= S \cap P^3 \cup (A \setminus S) \cap (A \setminus P^3) \\
&= \{\,0001, 0010, 0011, 0100, 1000, 1101, 1110, 1111\,\} \\
&\quad \cap \{\,0001, 0010, 0011, 0100, 0101, 1000, 1001, 1101, 1110, 1111\,\} \\
&\quad \cup \{\,0000, 0101, 0110, 0111, 1001, 1010, 1011, 1100\,\} \\
&\quad \cap \{\,0000, 0110, 0111, 1010, 1011, 1100\,\} \\
&= S \;\cup\; (A \setminus P^3) \\
&= \{\,0001, 0010, 0011, 0100, 1000, 1101, 1110, 1111\,\} \\
&\quad \cup \{\,0000, 0110, 0111, 1010, 1011, 1100\,\} \\
&= \mathbb{T}_4 \setminus \{\,0101, 1001\,\} \;.
\end{aligned}$$

From the equation 14 we obtain the numerical values of the equality degrees.

$$e(\chi_1, \chi) = 1 - \frac{2}{2^4} = \frac{7}{8}$$

$$e(\chi_2, \chi) = 1 - \frac{4}{2^4} = \frac{6}{8}$$

$$e(\chi_3, \chi) = 1 - \frac{2}{2^4} = \frac{7}{8} \ .$$

The results show, that the character on the Fig. 6 resembles the characters c_1 and c_3 on the Fig. 7 equally well, whereas the character c_2 a bit worse. Note, that we do not take into account the qualities q_i of the samples c_i when calculating the equality degrees.
Now we calculate the membership set $M(\chi, \pi)$ (U in terms of Theorem 5) and the membership value $m(\chi, \pi)$ of χ in π. We apply the equations 46–48.

$$\begin{aligned}
M(\chi, \pi) = U &= Q^1 \cap R^1 \cup Q^2 \cap R^2 \cup Q^3 \cap R^3 \\
&= Q^1 \cap m(Xq_1) \cup Q^2 \cap m(Xq_2) \cup Q^3 \cap m(Xq_3) \\
&= (\mathbb{T}_4 \setminus \{0011, 1111\}) \\
&\qquad \cap (\mathbb{T}_4 \setminus \{0111, 1010, 1011, 1101, 1110, 1111\}) \\
&\quad \cup (\mathbb{T}_4 \setminus \{0000, 0011, 1100, 1111\}) \\
&\qquad \cap (\mathbb{T}_4 \setminus \{0000, 0001, 0010, 0011, 0110, 0111, 1011, 1111\}) \\
&\quad \cup (\mathbb{T}_4 \setminus \{0101, 1001\}) \\
&\qquad \cap (\mathbb{T}_4 \setminus \{0000, 0001, 0010, 0100, 0101, 1000, 1001, 1100, 1101, 1110\}) \\
&= m(Xq_1) \setminus \{0011\} \cup m(Xq_2) \setminus \{1100\} \cup m(Xq_3) \\
&= \mathbb{T}_4 \ .
\end{aligned}$$

Clearly, by the Equation 12 and by the Lemma 1,

$$m(\chi, \pi) = 1 \ . \tag{59}$$

This means, that the sample χ perfectly matches the pattern π.

3.4 Discussion of the results

The interesting question that arises is what are the similarity degrees of each pattern element χ_i to the pattern π itself? It turns out that the pattern samples do not have to be of the best quality in order to assure that other input samples result in perfect matches.
We show that the membership sets $M(\chi_i, \pi)$ are proper subsets of $\mathbb{T}_4$ and therefore, the membership values $m(\chi_i, \pi)$ are less than 1 for all $i = 1, 2, 3$. We present the results of calculations only, leaving the details to the reader. Let us start with equality sets:

$$E(\chi_i, \chi_j) = \mathbb{T}_4 \setminus D(\chi_i, \chi_j) \ , \tag{60}$$

where $D(\chi_i, \chi_j)$ are the difference sets depicted on the Table 1.

$D(\chi_i, \chi_j)$	χ_1	χ_2	χ_3
χ_1	$\emptyset$	0000, 1100	0011, 0101, 1001, 1111
χ_2	0000, 1100	$\emptyset$	0000, 0011, 0101, 1001, 1100, 1111
χ_3	0011, 0101, 1001, 1111	0000, 0011, 0101, 1001, 1100, 1111	$\emptyset$

Table 1. Difference sets $D(\chi_i, \chi_j)$ for compound pattern elements

The matrix on the Table 1 is symmetric since $\chi_i \approx_p \chi_j$ is equivalent to $\chi_j \approx_p \chi_i$. Empty sets on the diagonal confirm, that $\chi_i \approx_p \chi_i$, for each $p \in \mathbb{T}_4$. We conclude that the equality values are as depicted on the Table 2.

$e(\chi_i, \chi_j)$	χ_1	χ_2	χ_3
χ_1	1	0.88	0.75
χ_2	0.88	1	0.62
χ_3	0.75	0.62	1

Table 2. Equality values $e(\chi_i, \chi_j)$ for compound pattern elements

Based on the above sets we calculate the membership sets and the membership values, similarly as before.

$$M(\chi_1, \pi) = \mathbb{T}_4 \setminus \{1111\} \qquad m(\chi_1, \pi) = 0.94 \ ,$$

$$M(\chi_2, \pi) = \mathbb{T}_4 \setminus \{0000, 1111\} \qquad m(\chi_2, \pi) = 0.88 \ ,$$

$$M(\chi_3, \pi) = \mathbb{T}_4 \setminus \{0101, 1001\} \qquad m(\chi_3, \pi) = 0.88 \ .$$

Thus, the similarity values of the characters c_1, c_2 and c_3 to the CCP built on top of them are 0.94, 0.88 and 0.88, respectively. None of them matches the pattern to the highest degree. Even though the membership values of χ_i in π are less than 1, there exist samples which match the CCP to the highest possible degree, with the membership value equal 1. Besides the character on the Fig. 6, the are three more – shown on the Fig.8 – for which the similarity degree reaches the maximal value.

	0001	0010	0011
0100			
1000			
1100	1101	1110	1111

	0001	0010	
0100			
1000			
1100	1101	1110	1111

	0001	0010	
0100			
1000			
	1101	1110	1111

Fig. 8. Three remaining samples with the best similarity to the pattern represented by χ.

Note, that the samples on the Fig. 6 and Fig. 8 differ only in pixels 0011 and 1100, which in at least one of the CCP elements on Fig. 7 belong to the sample and in at least another one belong to the background – being not excluded by the quality area at the same time.
The character samples c_i and their quality grades q_i were intentionally chosen so that they do not match the CCP to the highest degree, in order to demonstrate interpolation capabilities of the new mechanism. In typical cases, one constructs the CCP based on the good samples, which reflect most characteristics of the modelled pattern.

When creating a CCP one should bear in mind the following rule. Each pixel of the matrix must be covered by the foreground or background of at least one sample in the pattern. By covering we understand that it is included in at least one quality area. The reader may confirm that this rule is preserved in our example. If there exist a cell which is contained in exclusion area of each sample, then reaching the similarity value of 1 is not possible for any sample.

4. Conclusions

We demonstrated the method for character recognition based on metasets. The core of the idea lies in representing character samples and character patterns directly as metasets, as well as interpreting the membership and the equality degrees of corresponding metasets as the similarity degrees of characters. Although the idea is quite simple and straightforward, it seems to work fine. The experiments carried out with the computer application[1] implementing this model confirm that it adequately reflects human perception of similarity of characters. As we have seen, the mechanism requires some laborious calculations, however they are to be carried out by machines.

So far, no comparisons with other techniques for character recognition have been made. It must be stressed that the presented method is not by itself competitive to commercial solutions yet. It is rather a sketch of an idea which – when applied in cooperation with other techniques used for data processing, like centering and sharpening of character images – may turn out to have some advantages over other solutions.

The main goal of this chapter was to convince the reader, that the idea of metaset is applicable to solving problems related to processing of vague, imprecise data. And moreover, that modelling of real world using metasets is quite natural and simple. We showed that metaset membership correctly mimics similarity when characters are appropriately encoded.

It should be clear, that the discussed method has much wider scope of applications than recognition of letters. Although we presented the version for monochromatic (binary) images, it is not difficult to generalize it to color (many-valued) ones. The next step in research on the subject will focus on determining the characteristics of graphical data for which this method gives the best results.

5. References

Atanassov, K. T. (1986). Intuitionistic fuzzy sets, *Fuzzy Sets and Systems* 20: 87–96.

Kunen, K. (1980). *Set Theory, An Introduction to Independence Proofs*, number 102 in *Studies in Logic and Foundations of Mathematics*, North-Holland Publishing Company.

Pawlak, Z. (1982). Rough sets, *International Journal of Computer and Information Sciences* 11: 341–356.

Starosta, B. (2009). Application of metasets to character recognition, *Proc. of 18th International Symposium, ISMIS 2009*, Vol. 5722 of *Lecture Notes in Artificial Intelligence*, pp. 602–611.

Starosta, B. (2010). Representing intuitionistic fuzzy sets as metasets, *Developments in Fuzzy Sets, Intuitionistic Fuzzy Sets, Generalized Nets and Related Topics. Volume I: Foundations*, pp. 185–208.

Starosta, B. & Kosiński, W. (2009). *Views on Fuzzy Sets and Systems from Different Perspectives. Philosophy and Logic, Criticisms and Applications*, Vol. 243 of *Studies in Fuzziness and*

[1] The application is available as Java applet under the URL:
`http://www.pjwstk.edu.pl/~barstar/Research/MSOCR/index.html`

Soft Computing, Springer Verlag, chapter Meta Sets. Another Approach to Fuzziness, pp. 509–522.

Zadeh, L. A. (1965). Fuzzy sets, *Information and Control* 8: 338–353.

3

Recognition of Tifinaghe Characters Using Dynamic Programming & Neural Network

Rachid El Ayachi, Mohamed Fakir and Belaid Bouikhalene
Sultan Moulay Slimane University/
Faculty of Sciences and Techniques
Morocco

1. Introduction

Optical Character Recognition (OCR) is one of the most successful applications of automatic pattern recognition. The field of characters recognition is very important. Several studies have been conducted on Latin, Arabic and Chinese characters (Bozinovic and Shihari, 1989; Brown, 1983; Fakir and Sodeyama, 1993; Fakir, 2001; Chaudhuri and al, 2002; Blumenstein and al, 2002; Miyazaki and al, 1974; Mezghani and al, 2008; Lallican and al, 2000; Burr, 1982) and various commercial applications have been produced such as bank cheque processing, postal automation, documents. However, for Amazigh characters, called Tifinaghe, few studies have been published in the literature. Among these researches, we find (El ayachi and Fakir, 2009; Amrouch et al, 2009; Es saady, 2009; Fakir et al, 2009; El ayachi et al, 2010).
Because, characters are sensitive to noise the main problem in this field how to extracts strokes. This may be solved by the selection of the useful features customarily defined in the automatic character recognition as two types: global and local features. The principle of global features is based on the transformation of the character matrix into a new domain to extract features. The selection of local features is based on geometrical and topological properties of the character, such as strokes direction, strokes density, strokes length and position, etc.
Unlike Latin characters, Tifinaghe characters are formed by loops, lines and curves. This makes it difficult to describe a character in one parametric form. In this study, invariant moments, modified invariant moments and Walsh transform are used as features for the recognition of Tifinaghe characters. Fig.1 illustrates the block diagram of the proposed recognition system. Tifinaghe texts were transferred to the computer through an image scanner.
The process consists of three phases. After preliminary pre-processing of position normalization, noise reduction and skew correction), a text is segmented into lines and lines into what to be characters in the second phase. In the third phase features extraction methods are applied. In the last phase the recognition procedure is completed. In this phase a Multilayer Neural Network and Dynamic Programming Technique are used to classifier characters. These phases are described in the following sections, but before that a brief explanation about the characteristics of Tifinaghe characters is given.

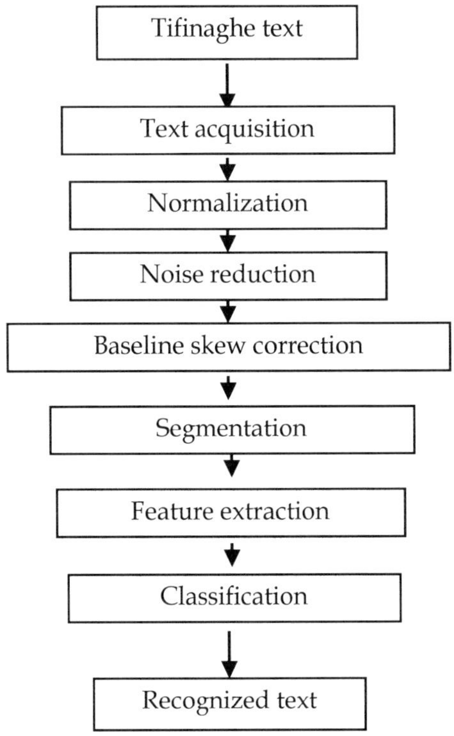

Fig. 1. Block diagram of the recognition system

2. Tifinaghe characters

The Tifinaghe script is used by approximately 20 million people who speak varieties of languages commonly called Berber or Amazigh. The three main varieties in Morocco are known as Tarifite, Tamazighe, and Tachelhite (El ayachi and Fakir, 2009; Es saady, 2009).
In Morocco, more than 40% of the population speaks Berber. In accordance with recent governmental decisions, the teaching of the Berber language, written in the Tifinaghe script, will be generalized and compulsory in Tifinaghe is an alphabetic writing system. It uses spaces to separate words and makes use of Western punctuation.
The earliest variety of the Berber alphabet is Libyan. Two forms exist: a Western form and an Eastern form. The Western variety was used along the Mediterranean coast from Kabylia to Morocco and most probably to the Canary Islands. The Eastern variety, old Tifinaghe, is also called Libyan-Berber or old Tuareg. It contains signs not found in the Libyan variety and was used to transcribe Old Tuareg (El ayachi and Fakir, 2009, rachidi, 2009).
Historically, Berber texts did not have a fixed direction. Early inscriptions were written horizontally from left to right, from right to left, vertically (bottom to top, top to bottom); boustrophedon directionality was also known. Modern-day Berber script is most frequently written in horizontal lines from left to right; therefore the bidirectional class for Tifinaghe letters is specified as strong left to right. Displaying Berber texts in other directions can be accomplished by the use of directional over rides or by the use of higher level protocols.
The encoding consists of four Tifinaghe character subsets: the basic set of the " Institut Royal de la Culture Amazighe (IRCAM) ", the extended IRCAM set, other Neo-Tifinaghe letters in

Character number	Character	Character number	Character	Character number	Character
1	ⴰ	12	ⵃ	23	ⵕ
2	ⴱ	13	ⵄ	24	ⵖ
3	ⴳ	14	ⵅ	25	ⵙ
4	ⴳⵯ	15	ⵇ	26	ⵚ
5	ⴷ	16	ⵉ	27	ⵛ
6	ⴹ	17	ⵊ	28	ⵜ
7	ⴻ	18	ⵍ	29	ⵟ
8	ⴼ	19	ⵎ	30	ⵡ
9	ⴽ	20	ⵏ	31	ⵢ
10	ⴽⵯ	21	ⵓ	32	ⵣ
11	ⵀ	22	ⵔ	33	ⵥ

Table 1. Tifinaghe characters adopted by IRCAM

use, and modern Tuareg letters. The first subset represents the set of characters chosen by IRCAM to unify the orthography of the different Moroccan modern day Berber dialects while using the historical Tifinaghe script.

The alphabet Tifinaghe adopted by IRCAM ([El ayachi and Fakir, 2009) is composed of thirty-three characters representing consonants and vowels as shown in Table 1. Fig.2 illustrates a Tifinaghe text.

Tifinaghe characters are consisted by loops, curves and lines segments. In addition some characters have the same shape which differs only by the addition of secondary parts (for example character 3&4, 10&9). This increases the complexity of recognizing Tifinaghe characters. Another problem is the rotation; some characters can be obtained from each other only by rotation of 90° (for example character 13&26, 19&30, 2&11) or 30° (example 23 & 26).

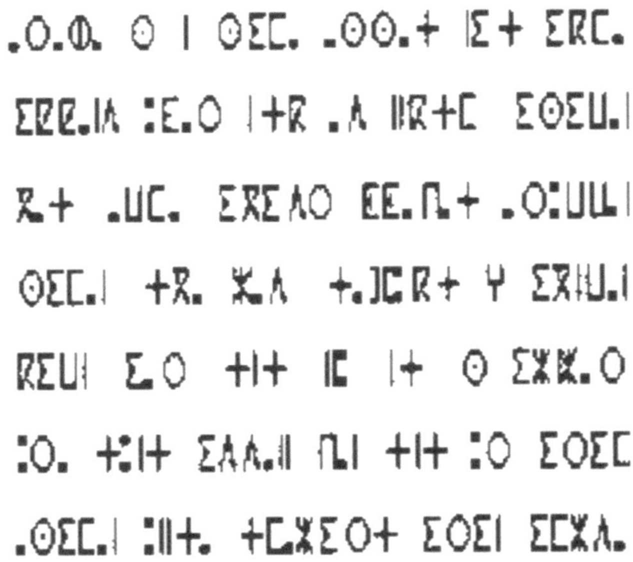

Fig. 2. An example of Tifinaghe text

3. Pre-processing

Pre-processing algorithms provides the required data suitable for further processing. In other words, it establishes the link between real word and recognition engine. Pre-processing steps consist of digitization of image document and cleaning it (by medium filter for example), converting the gray-scale image into binary image, normalizing the text (El ayachi et al, 2010), detecting and correcting baseline skew (Kayallieratou and al, 1999; Mnjunath et al, 2007), and segmenting (Casy et Lecolinet, 1996; Choisy et Belaid, 2002; Hadjar et Ingold, 2003) the text into lines and the lines into characters.

3.1 Normalization of the position

The position normalization is designed to eliminate unwanted areas and reduce the processing time. For this operation we use the histogram given by the following form:

$$HistV = \sum \sum pixel(x, y) \tag{1}$$

Where pixel(x, y), is the intensity of the pixel with the coordinates (x, y).
In this operation, firstly, we compute the horizontal and vertical histograms, secondly, we scan the horizontal histogram in two directions: from top to bottom and bottom to top respectively until the first meeting of black pixels, finally, we scan the vertical histogram in two directions: from left to right and right to left respectively until the first meeting of black pixels. After obtaining the positions of first black pixels, unwanted areas are eliminated in the image as shown in (Fig. 3).

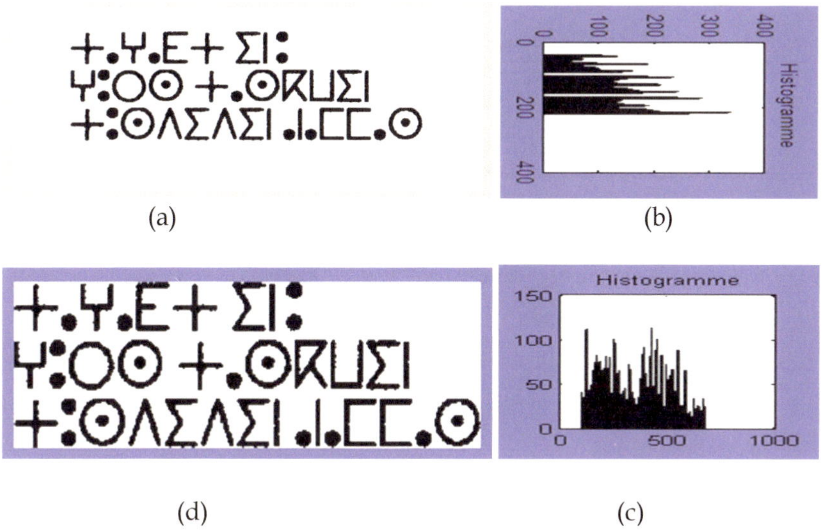

Fig. 3. (a) Before normalization, (d) after normalization, (b) Horizontal histogram and (c) Vertical histogram

3.2 Baseline skew detection and correction

In many document analysis systems, printed material is scanned and stored as an image. It is later retrieved for character and graphics extraction and recognition. During the scanning process, the document may be skewed and the text lines in the image may not be strictly horizontal. The skew may cause problems in text baseline extraction and document layout structure analysis. Several methods have been developed by many researchers for skew angle detection.

A skew angle is the angle that the text lines of the document image make with the horizontal direction. The skew correction is necessary for the success of many OCR systems. It consists of the extraction of the skew angle θs corresponding to baseline using Hough transform. The baseline is considered as the line corresponding to the maximum points in the horizontal projection profile. The skew angle θs is detected by observing high valued cell in the accumulative matrix in the Hough transform space. The image is then rotated by θs in the opposite direction so that the scripts become horizontal. Fig. 4(a) and Fig. 4(c) respectively show a text before and after baseline skew correction.

3.3 Segmentation

In this phase, the proposed OCR system detects individual text lines and then segments lines into characters. The lines of a text are segmented by using the horizontal histogram; we browse from top to bottom until the first line containing at least one black pixel, the line is the beginning of the first line of text, then we continue traverse until a line that contains only white pixels, this line corresponds to the end of the first line of text. With the same way, we continue to detect other text lines (Fig.5 a). The same principle is used in the vertical histogram to detect characters in each line of text (Fig.5 b).

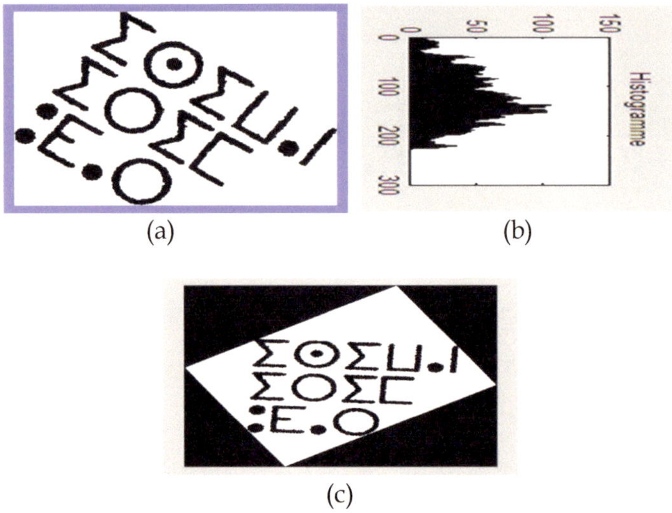

Fig. 4. (a) Before correction, (c) After correction and (b) Horizontal histogram

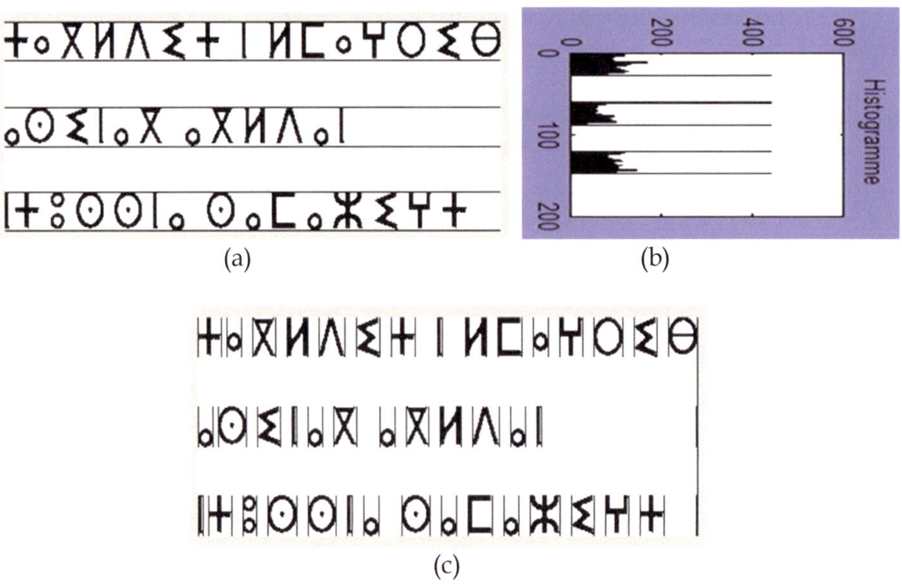

Fig. 5. (a) lines detection, (b) Horizontal histogram and(c) Characters segmentation

4. Features extraction

The next stage in the Tifinaghe character recognition is the feature extraction stage. Feature extraction represents the character image by a set of numerical features. These features are used by the classifier to classifier the data. In our work moments and other shape descriptors by Hu have been utilized to build the feature space. Using nonlinear combinations of geometric moments Hu derived a set of invariant moments which has the desired property of being invariant under image translation, scaling and rotation.

In addition to the invariant moments derived by Hu(Ibrahim, 2005), the modified invariant moments (Fakir and al, 2000), computed from the shape boundary for each character, and Walsh transform (Fazekas and Hajdu, 2001) are used as features.

4.1 Invariant moments

Let $f(x,y)$ be 1 over a closed and bounded region R and 0 otherwise. Define the $(p,q)th$ moment as:

$$m_{pq} = \iint_R x^p y^q f(x,y)dxdy \text{ , where } p,q = 0,1,2,... \tag{2}$$

The central moments can be expressed as

$$\mu_{pq} = \iint_R (x-\overline{x})^p (y-\overline{y})^q f(x,y)dxdy \tag{3}$$

Where

$$\overline{x} = \frac{m_{10}}{m_{00}} \text{ , } \overline{y} = \frac{m_{01}}{m_{00}} \tag{4}$$

However for digital images the continuous image intensity f(x,y) is replaced by a matrix where x and y are the discrete locations of the image pixels. The integral in equation 3 is approximated by the summation

$$\mu_{pq} = \sum_{(x,y)\in R} \sum (x-\overline{x})^p (y-\overline{y})^q f(x,y) \tag{5}$$

It can be verified that the central moments up to the order p+q≤ 3 may be computed by the following formulas:

$$\mu_{00} = m_{00} \tag{6}$$

$$\mu_{10} = 0 \tag{7}$$

$$\mu_{01} = 0 \tag{8}$$

$$\mu_{11} = m_{11} - \overline{y}m_{10} \tag{9}$$

$$\mu_{20} = m_{20} - \overline{x}m_{10} \tag{10}$$

$$\mu_{02} = m_{02} - \overline{y}m_{01} \tag{11}$$

$$\mu_{12} = m_{12} - 2\overline{y}m_{11} - \overline{x}m_{02} + 2\overline{y}^2 m_{10} \tag{12}$$

$$\mu_{21} = m_{21} - 2\overline{x}m_{11} - \overline{y}m_{20} + 2\overline{x}^2 m_{01} \tag{13}$$

$$\mu_{30} = m_{30} - 3\bar{x}m_{20} + 2\bar{x}^{2} m_{10} \tag{14}$$

$$\mu_{03} = m_{03} - 3\bar{y}m_{02} + 2\bar{y}^{2} m_{01} \tag{15}$$

The central moments are invariant to translation. They can also be normalized to be invariant to scaling change by the following formula. The quantities in equation (6) are called normalized central moments

$$\alpha_{pq} = \frac{\mu_{pq}}{\mu_{00}^{\gamma}} \tag{16}$$

Where

$$\gamma = \frac{p+q}{2} + 1 \quad \text{, for } p+q = 2,3,... \tag{17}$$

Invariant moments derived by Hu (Hu, 1962) were frequently used as features for shape recognition and were shown to be invariant to scaling, translation and rotation (Tables 2, 3, 4).

$$\varphi_1 = \alpha_{20} - \alpha_{02} \tag{18}$$

$$\varphi_2 = (\alpha_{20} - \alpha_{02})^2 + 4\alpha_{11}^2 \tag{19}$$

$$\varphi_3 = (\alpha_{30} - \alpha_{12})^2 + (3\alpha_{12} - \alpha_{03})^2 \tag{20}$$

$$\varphi_4 = (\alpha_{30} + \alpha_{12})^2 + (\alpha_{21} + \alpha_{03})^2 \tag{21}$$

$$\begin{aligned} \varphi_5 &= (\alpha_{30} - 3\alpha_{12})(\alpha_{30} + \alpha_{12})[(\alpha_{30} + \alpha_{12})^2 - 3(\alpha_{21} + \alpha_{03})^2] \\ &+ (3\alpha_{21} - \alpha_{03})(\alpha_{21} + \alpha_{03})[3(\alpha_{30} + \alpha_{12})^2 - (\alpha_{21} + \alpha_{03})^2] \end{aligned} \tag{22}$$

$$\begin{aligned} \varphi_6 &= (\alpha_{20} - \alpha_{02})[(\alpha_{30} + \alpha_{12})^2 - (\alpha_{21} + \alpha_{03})^2] \\ &+ 4\alpha_{11}(\alpha_{30} + \alpha_{12})(\alpha_{21} + \alpha_{03}) \end{aligned} \tag{23}$$

$$\begin{aligned} \varphi_7 &= (3\alpha_{21} - \alpha_{30})(\alpha_{30} + \alpha_{12})[(\alpha_{30} + \alpha_{12})^2 - 3(\alpha_{21} + \alpha_{03})^2] \\ &+ (3\alpha_{12} - \alpha_{03})(\alpha_{21} + \alpha_{03})[3(\alpha_{30} + \alpha_{12})^2 - (\alpha_{21} + \alpha_{03})^2] \end{aligned} \tag{24}$$

The φ_i's have dynamic values. Thus it was found that it was more practical to deal with the logarithm of magnitude of φ_i. Thus the seven moment invariants used in the proposed system are replaced by their logarithm values. For each character issued from the segmentation process the above moment invariant descriptors are calculated and fed to the classifiers.

$\log(\varphi_i)$	Original image 	Reduced image 	Mirror image 	Rotated image by (90°) 
φ_1	-1.3666	-1.3413	-1.3666	-1.3598
φ_2	-6.6891	-6.5944	-6.6891	-6.7362
φ_3	-7.1587	-7.3184	-7.1587	-7.3915
φ_4	-12.1029	-10.7623	-12.1029	-11.1215
φ_5	-24.2394	-20.1474	-24.2394	-20.4762
φ_6	-16.1004	-14.5595	-16.1004	-14.5128
φ_7	-22.1628	-21.5532	-21.7188	-21.2735

Table 2. Invariant Moments

$\log(\varphi_i)$	Original image 	Reduced image 	Mirror image 	Rotated image by (90°) 
φ_1	-1.5010	-1.5031	-1.5112	-1.5185
φ_2	-11.9233	-8.9845	-10.0586	-11.1259
φ_3	-7.7360	-7.7739	-7.4510	-7.3024
φ_4	-9.1054	-9.6056	-9.2274	-9.2739
φ_5	-17.9265	-18.5968	-17.9453	-17.9095
φ_6	-15.8471	-14.2235	-14.2585	-14.8929
φ_7	-18.6203	-19.4092	-18.9059	-18.7813

Table 3. Invariant Moments

$Log(\varphi_i)$		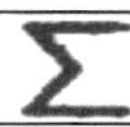	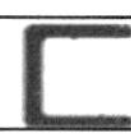	
φ_1	-1.2978	-1.5010	-1.7512	-1.5141
φ_2	-8.1338	-11.9233	-6.3559	-4.0690
φ_3	-12.2658	-7.7360	-14.2564	-8.4575
φ_4	-12.8021	-9.1054	-13.4338	-8.3696
φ_5	-25.3674	-17.9265	-27.6235	-16.8251
φ_6	-17.7442	-15.8471	-17.5999	-10.5131
φ_7	-27.0270	-18.6203	-27.5615	-16.9178

Table 4. Invariant Moments for different characters

4.2 Modified Invariant Moments

In this phase features are extracted from the external contour of the character (Fig.6). In order to differentiate between the characters illustrated in Fig.7that have the same external contour, we extract other features such C_ext, H_ext, V_ext, C_int, H_int and V_int , where

- C_ext is the number of externals contours;

- H_ext is the horizontal histogram. This feature is used to compute the number of externals contours;
- V_ext is the Vertical histogram. It is used to compute the number of externals contours;
- C_int is the number of internals contours;
- H_int is the horizontal histogram; it is used to compute the number of internals contours;
- V_int is the Vertical histogram; it is used to compute the number of internals contours.

Fig. 6. Tifinaghe characters Contours

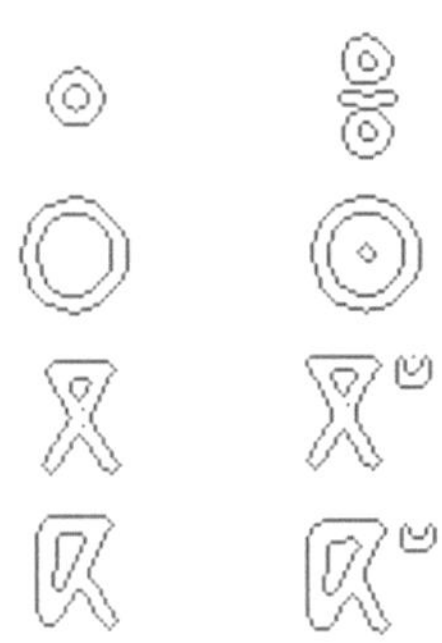

Fig. 7. Externals contours used to calculate modified invariant moments

We modified the moment definition in equation (2) using the character boundary only.

$$m_{pq} = \int_C x^p y^q f(x,y) ds \text{ , for p, q = 0, 1, 2, ...} \quad (25)$$

Where $\int_C$ is a line integral along the curve C, and

$$ds = \sqrt{((dx)^2 + (dy)^2)} \quad (26)$$

The modified central moments can be similarly defined as:

$$\mu_{pq} = \int_C (x - \bar{x})^p (y - \bar{y})^q ds \quad (27)$$

Where

$$\bar{x} = \frac{m_{10}}{m_{00}}, \quad \bar{y} = \frac{m_{01}}{m_{00}} \tag{28}$$

For a digital character, equation (9) becomes

$$\mu_{pq} = \sum_{(x,y)\in C} (x-\bar{x})^p (y-\bar{y})^q \tag{29}$$

The modified central moments are invariant to translation.
Theorem 1: For μ_{pq} defined in equation (9),

$$\alpha'_{pq} = \frac{\mu_{pq}}{(\mu_{00})^{p+q+1}} \text{ is scaling invariant for p, q = 2, 3, } \ldots \tag{30}$$

Proof: Suppose C is a smooth curve in the plane, C′ is the curve obtained homogeneously by rescaling the coordinates by a factor r, then

$$\mu'_{pq} = \int_C (x(s'))^p (y(s'))^q \, ds' = r^{p+q+1} \mu_{pq} \tag{31}$$

Since

$$\mu_{00} = \int_C ds = |C| = \text{length of curve C} \tag{32}$$

$$\mu'_{00} = \int_C ds' = |C'| = \text{ length of curve C}' = r \ |C| \tag{33}$$

Then, for any r > 0, we have

$$\frac{\mu'_{pq}}{(\mu'_{00})^{p+q+1}} = \frac{r^{p+q+1}\mu_{pq}}{r^{p+q+1}|C|} = \frac{\mu_{pq}}{(\mu_{00})^{p+q+1}} \tag{34}$$

The quantity in equation (34) is invariant to a homogenous scaling.
Theorem 2: Suppose C is a smooth curve in the plane and C′ is the curve obtained by rotating C an angle θ clockwise, then

$$\varphi'_i = \varphi_i \text{ for } 1 \leq \text{ i} \leq 7 \tag{35}$$

Where φ'_i is defined as in equations (18, 19, 20, 21, 22, 23 and 24) by using α'_{pq} instead of α_{pq} for $p+q=2,3,\ldots$
Proof:

$$\mu'_{pq} = \int_C (x(s'))^p (y(s'))^q \, ds' = \int_C \left\{ [x(s)\cos\theta - y(s)\sin\theta]^p \, [y(s)\sin\theta + x(s)\cos\theta]^q \right\} ds \tag{36}$$

Note that

$$ds' = ds \tag{37}$$

We shall prove $\varphi_1' = \varphi_1$ and $\varphi_2' = \varphi_2$ as examples.
For $3 \le j \le 7$,

$$\varphi_j' = \varphi_j \tag{38}$$

can be similarly proved after computations by using the trigonometric identities:

$$\cos^2\theta + \sin^2\theta = 1 \tag{39}$$

And

$$(\cos^3\theta - 3\cos\theta\sin^2\theta)^2 + (\sin^3\theta - 3\cos^2\theta\sin\theta)^2 = 1 \tag{40}$$

Table 5 represents the seven elements of the vector calculated using modified invariant moments for one character with four transformations.

$\log(\varphi_i)$				
φ_1	-0.0229	-0.0311	-0.0229	-0.0229
φ_2	-2.3107	-2.4123	-2.3107	-2.3107
φ_3	-3.4907	-3.5817	-3.4907	-3.4907
φ_4	-5.4983	-5.5664	-5.4983	-5.4983
φ_5	-10.2246	-10.3329	-10.2246	-10.2246
φ_6	-6.8287	-6.9195	-6.8287	-6.8287
φ_7	-10.6272	-10.7364	-10.6272	-10.3445

Table 5. Modified Invariant Moments

4.3 Walsh transform

The Walsh transformation is given by:

$$W(u,v) = \sum_{x=0}^{N-1}\sum_{y=0}^{N-1} f(x,y)g(x,y,u,v) \tag{41}$$

Where $f(x,y)$ is the intensity of the pixel with the coordinates (x,y) in the original binary image. The size of image f is $N * N$, and $u,v = 0,\ldots,N-1$, thus we compute N^2 Walsh transforms, $g(x,y,u,v)$ is the Kernel function given by the following form:

$$g(x,y,u,v) = (1/N)\prod_{i=0}^{n-1}(-1)^{b_i(x)b_{n-i-1}(u)+b_i(y)b_{n-i-1}(v)} \tag{42}$$

Where $b_i(x)$ is the ith bit in the binary expansion of x (it is equal either 0 or 1).
Table 6 represents the seven first elements of the vector Walsh calculated for one character with four transformations. While Table 7 illustrates Walsh coefficient calculated for different characters.

w_i				
w_1	-0.2500	-0.5000	-0.2500	-0.3750
w_2	-0.8750	-1	-0.8750	-1
w_3	-1.5000	-1.6250	-1.5000	-1.5000
w_4	-2.1250	-2.2500	-2.1250	-2.1250
w_5	-2.8750	-3	-2.8750	-2.8750
w_6	-3.3750	-3.6250	-3.5000	-3.6250
w_7	-3.8750	-4.1250	-4	-4.3750

Table 6. Walsh coefficients

w_i				
w_1	-0.0020	0	0	-0.0039
w_2	-0.0049	-0.0029	-0.0034	-0.0078
w_3	-0.0078	-0.0064	-0.0069	-0.0118
w_4	-0.0098	-0.0098	-0.0103	-0.0157
w_5	-0.0118	-0.0132	-0.0137	-0.0196
w_6	-0.0142	-0.0167	-0.0172	-0.0211
w_7	-0.0172	-0.0201	-0.0206	-0.0211

Table 7. Walsh coefficients

5. Characters recognition

In the character recognition system, the recognition is the last phase which is used to identify the segmented character. Where we use two techniques: the Neural Network (Hamza, 2008; Gu and al, 1983; Alnsour and Alzoubady, 2006; Asiri and Khorsheed, 2005) and Dynamic Programming (Sylvain and al, 2003).

5.1 Neural network

Characters are classified according to their computed features by means of artificial neural networks. Among the many applications that have been proposed for neural networks, character recognition has been one of the most successful. Many neural network architectures have been used in optical character recognition implementation. MLP is usually a common choice. Unfortunately, as the number of inputs and outputs grow, the MLP grows quickly and its training becomes very expensive. In addition, it is not easy to come up with a suitable network design and many trail-and-error cycles are required.

The Neural Network (Fig.8) represents an example of Multilayer Neural Network which contains one hidden layer. It has:

- An input layer of 7 (invariant moment's vector) inputs cells $E_i = X_i$ where the cells represents the inputs E_i of Network.
- A hidden layer of 3 activations Neural Y_j .
- An output layer of 6 activations Neural Z_k .
- 7×3 connections between input layer ant hidden layer, each weighted by V_{ji} .

- 3×6 connections between hidden layer and output layer, each weighted by W_{kj}.
- X_0, Y_0 are initialled values which are scalars.

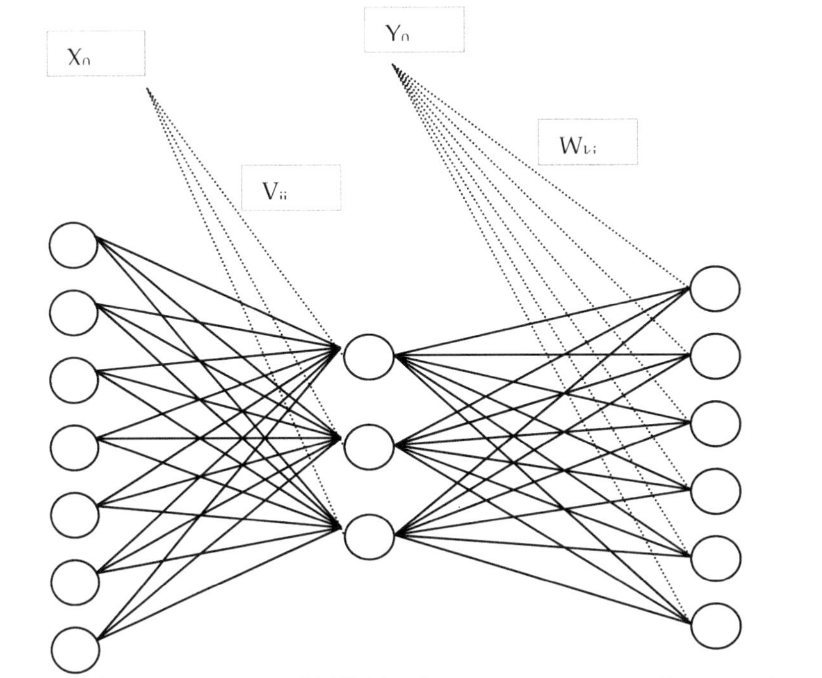

Fig. 8. Neural Network

The processing of Neural Network consists of five steps:

Step 1. Initializing of weights connections

The weights are randomly selected.

Step 2. inputs propagation

The inputs E_i are presented to input layer: $X_i = E_i$.

We propagate to hidden layer as follows

$$Y_j = f\left(\sum_{i=1}^{7} X_i V_{ji} + X_0\right) \tag{43}$$

After hidden layer, the output layer is given by

$$Z_k = f\left(\sum_{j=1}^{3} Y_j W_{kj} + Y_0\right) \tag{44}$$

where the values X_0 and Y_0 are scalars and f is the activation function given by

$$f(a) = 1 \big/ 1 + \exp(-a) \tag{45}$$

Step 3. Error back propagation

For each example of applied learning base input of the network, we calculate the error at output layers by the

$$E_k = Z_k(1 - Z_k)(S_k - Z_k) \tag{46}$$

where S_k desired output and Z_k the actual output.

In the next, we propagate this error on the hidden layer; the error of each neuron of the hidden layer is given by

$$F_j = Y_j(1 - Y_j)\sum_{k=1}^{6} W_{kj}.E_k \tag{47}$$

Step 4. Correction of connections weights

We change the weights connections as follows

- Between input layer and hidden layer:

$$\Delta V_{ji} = \eta.X_i.F_j \tag{48}$$

and

$$\Delta Y_0 = \eta.F_j \tag{49}$$

- Between hidden layer and output layer:

$$\Delta W_{kj} = \eta.Y_j.E_k \tag{50}$$

and

$$\Delta X_0 = \eta.E_k \tag{51}$$

Where $(\eta = 0.9)$ is the learning parameter determinate experimentally.

Step 5. (Loop)

Loop in step two allows computing the error threshold (0.0001), and the number of terations (50000).

After the learning of Network and the execution of Tifinaghe characters recognition system to recognize a text, we use the Euclidian distance to identify characters.

$$d(t_k, o) = \left(\sum_{i=1}^{6}(t_{ki} - o_i)^2\right)^{1/2} \tag{52}$$

With, t_k is a desired output and o is the output of Network.

5.2 Dynamic programming

Dynamic Programming was applied to speech recognition by Tappert et al 1982, by Sakoe and Chiba, 1978 to recognize Latin character and by El ayachi and al, 2010 to recognize Tifinaghe characters. The Dynamic Programming strategy is a useful technique for the problem of optimization. It is often used to find the shortest path from one place to another and solve the comparative problem between two strings.

The operation of Dynamic Programming (for invariant moments) is based on the following steps:

Step 1. Compute the matrix d between the vector of segmented character V_{car} and each one of the Tifinaghe characters vectors V_{ref} .
The matrix d is given by:

$$d(x,y) = \left|V_{car}(x) - V_{ref}(y)\right| \tag{53}$$

Where $x,y = 1,2,...,7$

Step 2. Calculate the optimal path from point $(1,1)$ to point (x,y) by the following recursive relationship:

$$S(x,y) = d(x,y) + \min\begin{Bmatrix} S(x-1,y), \\ S(x-1,y-1, \\ S(x,y-1) \end{Bmatrix} \tag{54}$$

Where
$S(x,y)$ is4 the cumulative distance along the optimal path from point $(1,1)$ to point (x,y).
$S(x,y)$ is eva4luated on the area $[1,7]*[1,7]$ that is browsed column by column or row by row starting from point $(1,1)$.

Step 3. Calculate the dissimilarity indices using the following form:

$$D(V_{car},V_{ref})=S(7,7)/7 \tag{55}$$

6. Experiments results

Experiments have been performed to test the above system. The developed Tifinaghe text recognition system has been tested on printed text. The system designed in Matlap for the recognition. The image to be tested is captured using a scanner. Before the recognition phase a database of 360 images is made. All tests are applied on 124 characters.
The system is working fine and showing a good recognition rate (Table 8). It has been noticed that the extracted features of the images produced from segmentation module deviate a lot from the respective results in the training set. It seems that the resolution differences are affecting the geometric moments of the image, making them highly variant. It is expected that the recognition rate of the system can be improved by normalizing the training set as the characters that result after the segmentation phase. The system has been implemented on Intel (R) Core (TM) 2 Duo, CPU T5870 @ 2.00 Ghz, with a RAM: 2.00 Go. The system is still under development.

	Dynamic Programming		Neural Network	
	Recognition rates	Error rates	Recognition rates	Error rates
Invariant Moments	93.55%	6.45%	94.35%	5.65%
Modified Invariant Moments	92.32%	7.68%	93.63%	6.37%
Walsh Transform	92.75%	7.25%	97.58%	2.42%

Table 8. Recognition rates & Error rates

7. Conclusion & perspectives

Two recognition methods based on neural network and dynamic programming has been presented. The system recognition consists of three phases including pre-processing, features extraction and recognition. The pre-processing includes position normalization, baseline skew correction and segmentation. The skew angle is determined by using Hough transform. The segmentation process consists of two steps: (a) segmentation of text into lines using horizontal histogram, (b) segmentation of lines into characters using vertical histogram. In features extraction phase a set of 7 invariant moments descriptors, 7 modified invariant moments descriptors and 7 Walsh coefficients have been used to represent the numerical features of the character extracted. Finally the numerical features are passed to the classifiers to recognize the character.

The programs were written using Matlap. As mentioned previously, no efficient technique has been found for Tifinaghe scripts recognition. This field is of importance for future research.

8. References

Alnsour, A.J. and L.M. Alzoubady. (2006). *Arabichandwritten characters recognized by neocognitron artificial neural network*. J. Pure Appl. Sci., 3: 1- 17.

Asiri, A. and M.S. Khorsheed. (2005). *Automatic processing of handwritten Arabic forms using neural networks*. Proceeding of the World Academy of Science, Engineering and Technology, Aug. 2005, pp: 313-317.

Attila Fazekas and Andras Hajdu. (2001). *Recognizing Type set Documents using Walsh*, JCIT-CIT 9, 2-2001, pp: 101-112.

B B Chaudhuri, U Pal and M Mitra. (2002). *Automatic recognition of printed Oriya script*, Sädhanä Vol. 27, Part 1, February 2002, pp. 23–34. © Printed in India.

Casey & Lecolinet . (1996). *A survey of methods and strategies in character segmentation*. IEEA Transactions on Pattern Analysis and Machine Intelligence, Vol. 18, No. 7, pp: 690-706 July 1996.

Ch. Choisy and A. Belaid. (2002). *Cross- learning in analytic word recognition without segmentation*, in Int. Journal on documentAnal. & Recognition IJDAR, 4(4): 281-289, 2002

C. Tappert. (1982). *Cursive Script Recognition by Elastic Matching*, IBM J. Res. Develop., Vol. 26, No. 6, 1982, pp. 765-771.

D. J. Burr. (1982). *A Normalizing Transform For Cursive Script Recognition*, Proc. 6th Int. J. Conf. on Pattern Recognition Munich (1982), pp. 1027–1030.

E.Kavallieratou, N.Fakotakis, and G.Kokkinakis. (1999). *Skew Angle Estimation in Document Processing Using Cohen's Class Distributions*, PRL(20), No. 11-13, November 1999, pp. 1305-1311.

Hadjar, K. and R. Ingold. (2003). *Arabic newspaper segmentation*. Proceeding of 7th International Conference on Document Analysis and Recognition, Aug. 3-6, IEEE Computer Society, pp: 895-899.

Hamza, Ali A. (2008). *Back Propagation Neural Network Arabic Characters Classification Module Utilizing Microsoft Word*; Journal of Computer Science 4 (9): 744-751, 2008.

H. Sakoe and S. Chiba. (1978). *Dynamic Programming Algorithm Optimization for Spoken Word Recognition*, IEEE Trans. Acoust., Speech and Signal Processing, Vol. ASSP-26, No. 1, 1978, pp. 401-408

Ibrahim S. I. Abuhaiba. (2005). *Arabic Font Recognition Using Decision Trees Built From Common Words*, JCIT-CIT 13, 3-2005, 211-223

M. Amrouch, Y. Es saady, A. Rachidi, M. El Yassa and D. Mammass. (2009). *Printed Amazigh Character Recognition by a Hybrid Approach Based on Hidden Markov Models and the Hough Transform*, 978-1-4244-3757-3/09/$25.00 ©2009 IEEE

M. Blumenstein & C. K. Cheng & X. Y. Liu. (2002). *New Preprocessing Techniques for Handwritten Word Recognition*, in Proceedings of the Second IASTED International Conference on Visualization, Imaging and Image Processing (VIIP 2002), ACTA Press, Calgary, pp. 480-484.

M. Fakir. (2001). *Reconnaissance des Caractères Arabes Imprimés*, Thesis, 2001, pp : 28-36.

M. Fakir, B. Bouikhalene and K. Moro. (2009). *Skeletonization Methods Evaluation for the Recognition of PrintedTifinaghe characters*, SITCAM'09, Agadir-Maroc

M. Fakir and C. Sodeyama. (1993). *Recognition of Arabic printed Scripts by Dynamic Programing Matching Method*, IECICE Trans. Inf & Syst, Vol. E76- D, No.2 Feb. 93, pp: 31-37

M. Fakir, M.M. Hassani and C.Sodeyama. (2000). *On the recognition of Arabic characters using Hough transform technique*, Malysian Journal of Computer Science Vol. 13, No.2, Dec.2000, pp: 39-47.

M. K. Brown. (1983). *Pre-processing techniques for cursive word recognition*, Pattern Recognition, Vol.13, N°.5, pp: 447-451, 1983

M. K. Hu. (1962). *Visual pattern recognition by moment invariants*, IRE trans. Infor. Theory TT-8, pp: 179-187, 1962.

Mnjunath Aradhya et al. (2007). *Skew estimation technique for binary document images based on thinning and moments*, engineering letters, 14:1, EL_14_1_22, 2007.

N. Mezghani, A.Cheret and N.Mitiche. (2008). *Bayes classification of online arabic characters by Gibbs modeling of class conditional densities*, IEEE Trans PAMI Vol 30, issue 7, july 2008, pp: 1121-1131

N. Miyazaki et al. (1974). *Recognition of handprint katakana characters*, Annual conference of inf. Process. Society of Japan, 1974.

P.M. Lallican, C. Viarp-Gaudin, S. Knerr. (2000). *From off-line to on-line handwriting recognition*. Proc. 7th workshop on frontiers in handwriting recognition, pp.303-312, Amsterdam 2000.

R. El ayachi and M. Fakir. (2009). *Recognition of Tifinaghe Characters Using Neural Network*, 978-1-4244-3757-3/09/$25.00 ©2009 IEEE

R. El ayachi, K. Moro, M. Fakir and B. Bouikhalene. (2010). *On The Recognition Of Tifinaghe Scripts*, JATIT, vol. 20, No. 2, pp: 61-66, 2010.

R. M. Bozinovic and S. N. Shihari. (1989). *Off Line Cursive Script Word Recognition*, IEEE Trans.Pattern Anal. Mach. Intell. PAMI 11, 1989, pp. 68- 83

Sylvain Chevalier, Edouard Geoffrois, and Franc¸oise Prêteux. (2003). *A 2D Dynamic Programming Approach for Markov Random Field-based Handwritten Character Recognition*, Proceedings IAPR International Conference on Image and Signal Processing (ICISP' 2003), Agadir, Morocco, 2003, p. 617-630.

Y. Es saady, M.Amrouch, A. Rachidi, M. El Yassa and D. Mammass. (2009). *Reconnaissance de caractères Amazighes Imprimés par le Formalisme des Automates à états finis*, SITCAM'09, Agadir-Maroc,12-13 December 2009, pp:48-57.

Y.X. Gu et al. (1983). *Application of a multilayer tree in computer recognition of Chinese character*, IEEE Trans. On PAMI-5, N°.1, pp: 83-89, 1983.

4

Character Degradation Model and HMM Word Recognition System for Text Extracted from Maps

Aria Pezeshk and Richard L. Tutwiler
Applied Research Lab, The Pennsylvania State University
USA

1. Introduction

Geographic maps are one of the most abundant and valuable sources of accurate information about various features of bodies of land and water. Due to their importance in applications ranging from city planning and navigation to tracking changes in vegetation cover and coastline erosion, most countries have established dedicated organizations that are responsible for the production and maintenance of maps that cover their entire territories. This has resulted in the production and availability of a tremendous quantity of useful information about every part of the world.

As with other types of documents, new maps are nowadays produced in specialized computer programs, and are easy to manage and update since the individual information layers that form the whole map are available to the map producer. In addition to the change in the method of production, the applications and ways to process maps have also changed in the past few decades. Geographic Information Systems (GIS) have provided new means to analyze, process, visualize, and integrate various forms of geographic data. The input to these systems can be satellite or aerial imagery, remote sensing data (e.g. LIDAR images), raster or vector representations of geographic maps, and any other type of data that are related to locations (e.g. local populations, crime statistics, and textual information). Due to their wide availability, accuracy, and relative cheapness compared to other types of geo-referenced data, geographic maps are probably the most widely used source of information for GIS users. However, the majority of existing geographic maps exist only in printed form. This means that unlike the case for computer generated maps, printed maps cannot be directly used as the input to a GIS since both the end users and the map producers only have access to the dense and complex mixture of regularly intersecting and/or overlapping set of graphical and textual elements rather than the individual features of interest.

Currently the only reliable way of converting printed maps into computer readable format is to have a highly trained operator manually extract the individual sets of features (graphical and textual). The manual feature extraction methods consist of digitization using a digitizing tablet, and heads-up digitizing. In the first method, the paper map is placed on top of the digitizing tablet, and the operator traces over lines and other objects of interest using a stylus or a digitizing puck (a device with crosshairs and multiple buttons that enable data entry operations). In heads-up digitizing (otherwise known as on-screen digitizing) on the other hand, the paper map is first scanned into a digital image. The operator then traces over every single object of interest on the computer screen using a mouse. Since zooming into difficult sections of the map and editing capabilities are supported in this case, heads-up digitizing is now the more popular method for digitizing the graphical features in paper maps. In addition to the graphical elements, the textual content of maps also needs to be manually extracted and assigned to the appropriate objects in the digital copy. Manual conversion of maps into usable digital format is therefore a tedious, labor intensive, and error prone process. While these procedures may be viable for small scale operations that only involve a few maps, they are unpractical for large scale conversion of whole map repositories. A system that can automate this process is therefore essential for GIS users to replace the manual map conversion methods and provide them with easy access to the vast number of printed maps that exist in various archives and produced by different organizations around the globe.

In this chapter we discuss a custom recognition system for text extracted from maps. This work is part of a larger system that enables automatic sequential extraction of various graphical features, and subsequently processes the remaining image for text grouping, reorientation, and extraction (Pezeshk & Tutwiler, 2008a;b; 2010b). The recognition engine presented here extends the application of the system we developed in (Pezeshk & Tutwiler, 2010a) by enabling multi-font and segmentation-free recognition.

We focus on this particular problem because unlike other parts of the map conversion process, text recognition has received little attention in the research carried out in the field of automatic map understanding systems (as will be discussed in Section 3). Moreover, the level of noise and deformities in text extracted from maps can be too severe for commercial Optical Character Recognition (OCR) systems, resulting in low recognition rates and thereby higher user involvement in correcting the errors in post processing.

The system proposed here can find a variety of applications. Combined with our previous work in (Pezeshk & Tutwiler, 2008a;b; 2010b), we obtain a complete map understanding system that can digitize both the graphical and textual content of printed maps. Since both types of features are extracted at the same time, the text recognized using our system can easily be associated with the other digitized objects in the image (e.g. road labels with the corresponding road segments) in order to obtain an exact digital representation. Moreover, the recognized text can be entered into a database and used to search for maps that contain a particular street or area of interest, or to classify map archives in a similar manner according to their text content. Since geographic maps are accurately geo-referenced, the text can also be used in conflation with satellite or aerial imagery to automatically tag locations or objects that exist in these types of images.

The remainder of this chapter is organized as follows. First, in Section 2 we discuss the challenges encountered in the extraction and recognition of the text content of scanned maps. A brief overview of research in the fields of document image analysis and map conversion algorithms is then presented in Section 3. Details of the different components of our text recognition system which include a custom noise model for the generation of artificial training sets, preprocessing algorithm for automatic text size normalization and orientation correction, and the Hidden Markov Model (HMM) based text recognition engine are subsequently discussed in Sections 4.2, 4.3, and 4.4, respectively. Finally, experimental results are shown in Section 5 before concluding the chapter in Section 6.

2. Challenges

Geographic maps are designed to convey the largest possible amount of information and details regarding both the natural features (e.g. rivers and vegetation cover) and manmade structures (e.g. roads and major buildings) that are located on any given expanse of land or water. Topographic maps go a step further and incorporate three dimensional topography data which are represented by contour lines. The superposition of the various graphical features and the textual information that is used to label them onto a single two dimensional document results in a complex mixture in which the feature layers (graphical or textual) are regularly intersecting and/or overlapping with each other and thereby no longer individually accessible. Moreover, the common existence of colored or textured backgrounds in maps means that the range of colors that can be used for the various objects in the foreground is limited to only a handful of colors (typically brown, black, blue, and green) in order to maintain their readability. Hence in most cases the same color is used to represent more than one type of feature. While the human visual system is fully capable of discerning each individual type of feature, the density and regular intersections between the different constituent layers of a geographic map comprise the primary challenges in extracting its textual content.

Scanning artifacts such as blurring, aliasing, and mixed color pixels further complicate the text extraction process and its subsequent recognition by affecting the integrity of features in the map image (Khotanzad & Zink, 2003). Geographic maps are particularly susceptible to scanning artifacts since both the graphical features such as roads and contour lines, and the text consist of thin linear segments that are more severely affected by the blending of colors across adjacent pixels and erosion of the edges.

The recognition of the text content of geographic maps has its own set of difficulties. Due to the lack of direct access to the text layer, the graphical features need to be extracted first. As each of these features have distinct characteristics, several processing steps (such as color processing, binarization, and morphological operations) are required to sequentially extract each type of feature until a text only image can be obtained. Misclassification errors that place character segments in any of the graphics layers, or misidentify parts of non-text objects (such as line fragments from the road layer) as belonging to the text layer can result in mild to severe levels of noise and defects in the extracted characters. Furthermore, the text only image will still need to undergo additional processing to group the characters into their respective strings and reorient them to the horizontal direction. Reorientation errors are thus another possible challenge that can cause problems for the segmentation of whole words into individual characters and the recognition of the text.

Text recognition is a well studied subject and is considered a solved problem for the majority of end users who only need to process regular high quality office documents. However, the recognition rates of commercial OCRs are known to drop significantly in the presence of less than ideal conditions (Baird, 2007). Degradations to the quality of the extracted characters that are due to the accumulation of errors from the various processing steps will therefore require the development of a custom text recognition system that is specifically designed and trained according to the anticipated types and levels of defects present in this type of text.

3. Document Image analysis & map conversion systems: A brief overview

The term document image analysis is referred to any set of algorithms and systems that are concerned with the automatic interpretation of printed or handwritten documents. While nearly every new document or drawing is generated by computer software, there is still an immense amount of archived printed material such as engineering drawings, blueprints, microfiches, and maps that need to be converted into machine readable format. Many other types of documents such as checks and forms that are filled by hand on a regular basis also need to be eventually processed by a computer system so that their content can be transmitted more easily or electronically filed. Document analysis has therefore been an active area of research since the early days of image processing and computer vision.

In forms and checks the graphical elements serve to provide reserved spaces for the text, or act as separators between different parts of these documents. As a result the graphical objects (such as rectangular enclosures, straight lines, and logos) which do not provide any useful information can be simply detected and removed using common line detection algorithms (e.g. Hough transform) or basic morphological operations, and the main steps in the processing of such documents will typically consist of skew correction (so that the extracted strings are correctly reoriented to the horizontal direction) and handwritten text recognition (Hull, 1998), (Sarfraz et al., 2005), (Guillevic & Suen, 1997), (Namane et al., 2006).

Engineering drawings and blueprints contain a large amount of information presented as both text and graphics. Therefore both types of features need to be extracted with high accuracy and the tolerance level for misclassification errors is low. However, text and graphics rarely intersect with each other, and the two classes of features can be typically separated from each other using connected component analysis (graphical features tend to be larger in pixel area than characters). Smaller graphical features in such documents mostly consist of arrows, dashed lines, and hatched areas. As the general shapes and characteristics of such objects are known beforehand, specialized modules can be subsequently applied to the image to obtain a text only image. Therefore the separation of the graphical elements has little effect on the integrity of the extracted text layer, and both commercial and custom OCR systems can be used for its recognition. These conditions have led to the development of many practical digitization systems (Tombre et al., 2002), (Dori & Wenyin, 1999), (Lu, 1998), (Wenyin et al., 2007), (Chen et al., 1999).

Due to the difficulties associated with the extraction of features from geographic maps in general, and topographic maps in particular, many of the systems presented in the literature have focused on simpler maps where features are well separated from each other or printed in colors that facilitate the map digitization process (e.g. see (Pouderoux et al., 2007), (Roy et al., 2007)). Other systems mostly consider the extraction of one or more types of features from complex maps ((Chiang et al., 2005; Dhar & Chanda, 2006; Gamba & Mecocci, 1999; Kerle & Leeuw, 2009; Khotanzad & Zink, 2003; Leyk et al., 2006)), but do not address the problems of non-horizontal text or character recognition.

Cao et al. (Cao & Tan, 2002) used a commercial OCR to recognize text extracted from street maps that have limited intersection between different features. Li et al. (Li et al., 2000) rely on a cooperative method to extract graphical features from complex maps. An OCR that uses template matching and trained using actual character prototypes that are manually labeled is then used to recognize the text. Velázquez and Levachkine (Velázquez & Levachkine, 2003) assume most of the graphical features can be removed using binarization of the original image. A method called V-lines is subsequently used to separate the text in the remaining image from possible attached artifacts or symbols. The extracted text is finally recognized using an artificial neural network in conjunction with a gazetteer. Similar recognition systems have been reported in (Levachkine et al., 2002) and (Gelbukh et al., 2003).

In the next section we discuss our proposed approach that aims to minimize the required amount user involvement in the extraction of the text content and overcome the challenges encountered in character recognition for topographic maps.

4. Proposed system

4.1 Text extraction

The text extraction procedure involves the sequential application of several modules that perform text/graphics separation, followed by text grouping and reorientation as shown in Figure 1. The particular set of procedures discussed here are primarily targeted at topographic maps produced by the United States Geological Survey (USGS) since they encompass many of the difficulties discussed in Section 2 such as variety and density of features, and usage of the same color for several of the intersecting features. The different components of the text extraction system are designed to contain easily adjustable parameters, and to have minimal reliance on heuristics and prior knowledge about the underlying map image. The extension of the proposed algorithms to maps produced by other organizations can then be easily achieved by proper selection of these parameters. Here we assume that the individual binary word images that constitute the input to our recognition system are already extracted using this multi step process. We therefore provide only a high level description of its different elements below and refer the interested reader to the related publications for details of each algorithm:

- *Contour Line Extraction*: Contour lines are first extracted based on their color property. However, due to the mixed color pixel problem (as mentioned in Section 2) the raw colors in the original image cannot be used. Instead, we use the algorithm in (Pezeshk & Tutwiler, 2008a) to create a false color image in which the intra-cluster variance of colors of contour line pixels has been reduced. A sample patch containing only contour line pixels is then manually selected, and a distance threshold computed according to the statistics of the sample points is used to extract the contour lines. A similar procedure can be repeated for any other type of feature that is printed in color (such as rivers). The remaining image consisting only of features printed in black (such as roads, text, and man made structures) is subsequently binarized.
- *Linear Feature Extraction*: Roads and boundary lines only gradually change directions, and can be considered to be piecewise straight or nearly straight. The algorithm presented in (Pezeshk & Tutwiler, 2010b) extracts such linear features based on this observation. Analogous to the process of describing a vector in terms of a number of basis vectors, the input binary image is dissected into multiple directional feature planes which contain the projections of the edges of every object towards a number of primary directions. Due to the aforementioned "straightness" property, every line will have one or more projections in the directional planes that are longer than edge projections from character segments and other non-line objects. A set of directional morphological operations that operate on non-isotropic neighborhoods are subsequently used to automatically eliminate these shorter edge projections, and to reconstruct whole lines from the remaining core edge segments. The linear feature layer is then defined as the union of the restored line segments from all the directional planes, and extracted from the image. This directional line extraction method has the benefit of being capable of extracting lines even when they are intersecting with the text layer, while causing minimal damage to the integrity of the characters.
- *Clutter Removal*: The remaining non text objects consisting of buildings, dashed lines, and line fragments are removed using morphological operations, a dashed line detection algorithm, and a search process that identifies isolated linear artifacts, respectively (Pezeshk & Tutwiler, 2008b; 2010b).

- *Text Grouping & Reorientation*: Grouping of characters into their respective strings is performed using pyramid decomposition with Gaussian kernels. Going down through the consecutive levels of the pyramid, the successive downsampling and smoothing cause adjacent characters to merge together. When the image is upsampled to its original size and binarized, the general area of each string can be identified by the blobs formed in the upsampled image. Individual strings can then be reoriented to the horizontal direction according to the orientation of the longer edge of the minimum area enclosing rectangle fitted onto each of the blobs (Pezeshk & Tutwiler, 2010b). Examples of the extracted text are shown in Figure 2.

4.2 Noise model

Text recognition systems can in general be divided into two categories. Those in the first group rely on a segmentation algorithm (see e.g. (Casey & Lecolinet, 1996)) to obtain the individual characters in every word image, and then send each of the extracted characters to a classifier trained on single character images for recognition. The performance of such systems is mainly determined by the accuracy of the segmentation procedure. As seen in Figure 2, words extracted from maps may contain broken and/or conjoined characters, and italicized typeface, which are all conditions that lead to a higher likelihood for segmentation errors. The cascading effect of such errors coupled with the difficulties in recognizing characters with mild to severe levels of noise and defects will consequently result in unacceptable overall performance rates.

One of the most promising approaches for the recognition of heavily noisy or degraded characters belongs to the second general category of recognition systems that do not rely on prior segmentation of a word image into its constituent characters. Kuo et al. (Kuo & Agazzi, 1994) and Aggazi et al. (Agazzi et al., 1993) obtained excellent recognition results for severely degraded word images using pseudo two dimensional HMMs that modeled all or major parts of words which were known to belong to a small sized lexicon. The training procedure for these systems would therefore also consist of images of whole or major parts of the known words. Since the text in maps mainly consists of names that may not be known a priori, using such an approach is not possible in this case.

Here we use a procedure that relies on implicit segmentation of the word images into individual characters, followed by recognition using a combination of classifiers. Similar to the segment-then-recognize systems, the training data for our recognition engine will therefore consist of single character images.

Large scale experiments have shown that the dominant factors in determining the performance of text recognition systems are the size and representativeness of their training data (Baird, 2007). The ideal set of training images in our application would therefore consist of actual single character images that have been extracted from real maps. However, geographic maps only contain a small amount of text that is difficult to extract and label, and appears in multiple different fonts. The collection of enough number of real character samples for training would therefore require processing many different map sheets, which in addition to being very difficult and time consuming, may not be possible if a large number of maps with similar features are not available. We therefore propose using a custom noise model that replicates the types of defects and deformations seen in actual characters extracted from maps, and allows us to generate training sets with arbitrary size.

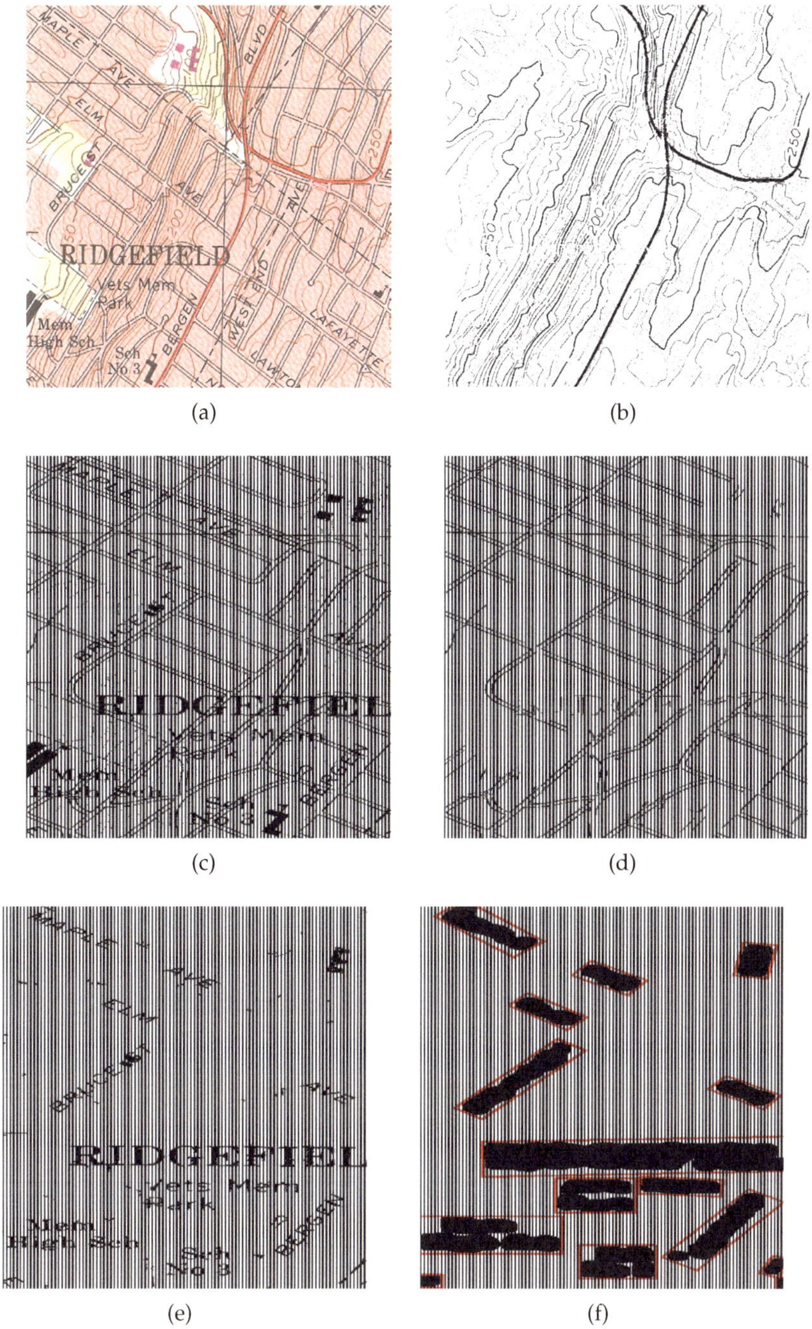

Fig. 1. Performance evaluation of the text and graphics separation modules; (a) Original map image, (b) Extracted Contour Lines, (c) Foreground image, (d) Extracted linear features , (e) Text image, (f) Grouped characters and their respective minimum area enclosing rectangles

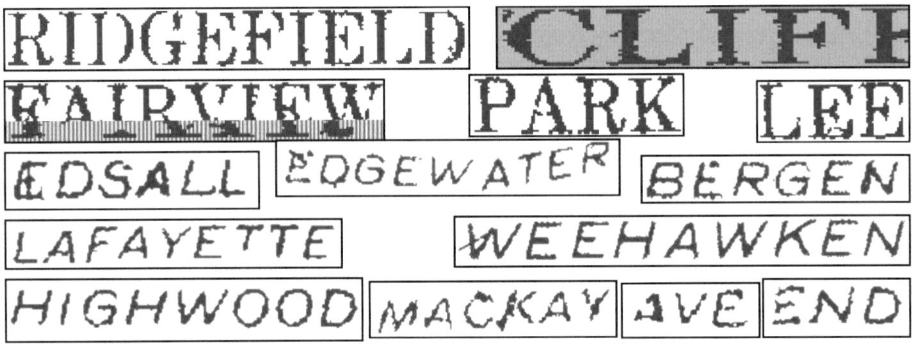

Fig. 2. Samples of extracted words

We use the degradation model introduced by Baird (Baird, 1992) as the starting point of our defect model. Instead of the full model, here we pick the following four types of degradations that were deemed to be most relevant to our application:

- *Spatial Quantization*: A degradation that is a function of character size (in units of points) and scanning resolution (in pixels/inch).
- *Blurring*: Deformations caused by the combined effect of the point spread functions of the printing and scanning processes are modeled by the parameter *blur* (in units of output pixels) which is defined as the standard error of a circularly symmetric 2D Gaussian filter.
- *Speckle Noise*: Per-pixel additive noise is modeled by the parameter *sens* (in units of intensity) which is defined as the standard error of a normal distribution with zero mean. This parameter models the side effects of the color transformation used in the contour line removal step.
- *Thresholding*: Effects of binarization of the map image are modeled using the parameter *thresh* (in units of intensity, assuming white and black are represented by 0 and 1 respectively).

To generate an artificial character image using this model, which we refer to as the Truncated Defect Model (TDM), a noise free binary image of the desired character is first rendered at around ten times the output resolution. This image is then shifted randomly within [0,1] (in output pixel units) in the horizontal and vertical directions, blurred, and subsampled to output resolution. Per pixel speckle noise is subsequently added to this image, and the whole image is binarized using the parameter *thresh*.
Another type of artifact that can be found Figure 2 are short linear attachments that were originally parts of intersecting lines. The model above is thus supplemented by a random linear artifact generator that replicates this type of artifact using an iterative procedure, and allows for complete randomization and parametrization of the direction, connectivity, point of origin, length, and width of line attachments for character images. The details of this model which we refer to as the Extended Defect Model (EDM) are as follows:

Step 1) *Initialization*: Assuming uniform distribution over the range of possible values for each parameter, the defining attributes of the linear artifact are randomly selected during initialization. First, an initial growth point G_0 is randomly selected from the pixels on the perimeter of a character image generated by the TDM. Due to the relatively short length of the linear artifacts, they can be assumed to be straight or nearly straight. Hence

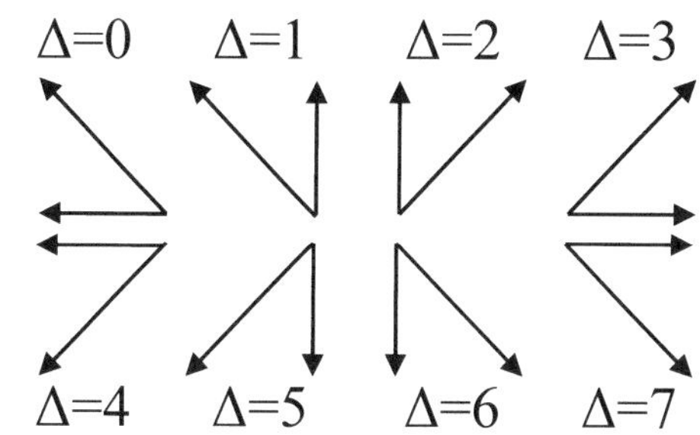

Fig. 3. Possible growth directions from a previous pixel

the second random selection picks one of the eight combined directions in Fig. 3 as the general direction of growth for all subsequent iterations. Each direction Δ identifies two candidate directions of growth and therefore two new neighboring pixels at each iteration. The selection of one of these two candidate growth pixels is performed based on the probability pair $(p, 1-p)$ in each iteration, where the value of p is picked randomly during initialization from $V_p = [0.1, 0.2, \ldots, 0.8, 0.9]$. Finally, the parameter L_{seg} is randomly selected from the vector $V_L = [2, 4, \ldots, L_{max}]$ to determine the total length (in number of pixels) of the generated line segment.

Step 2) *Growth*: At each iteration t, one of the two neighboring pixels N_1 and N_2 of the previous growth location G_{t-1} is randomly selected based on the probability pair $(p, 1-p)$ as the new growth pixel G_t. Discontinuities along the intersecting line fragments are then replicated by using a second random process to determine whether G_t will be an ON (or OFF) pixel (in other words 1 or 0, respectively) with probability q (or $1-q$). The direction orthogonal to current direction of growth at each iteration is along the line's width. Linear artifacts that are more than one pixel thick can therefore be obtained using the same general procedure, but at each iteration one or more pixels should be added (grown) along the width of the line.

Step 3) *Stopping criteria*: Continue until $t = L_{seg}$

4.3 Text normalization

The feature vectors that are used as the input to the recognition engine should all have the same length. Every extracted word image thus needs to be normalized to a fixed height according to the desired length of feature vectors. Under normal circumstances, the height of individual characters are accurate indicators of the actual font size, and thereby the normalization factor. However, due to the presence of attached artifacts that may extend above or below the actual boundaries of characters, noise and defects, and possible deviations in orientation from the horizontal, the actual character size cannot be inferred based on the heights of characters here. Instead, we use a custom preprocessing algorithm to normalize words printed in either lower case or upper case to the appropriate target size.

Words printed in upper case can be considered to be encased between two imaginary lines that pass through the tops and bottoms of its constituent characters. Estimation of these lines, named cap line and baseline, respectively, should therefore enable us to find the actual bounds of characters and thereby correctly normalize each and every whole word image to the desired size.

Similar to any other regression problem, we first need to select a source of data, and an estimation algorithm. Since the word images are horizontal or nearly horizontal, we can use the pixels located on the outer contours of characters as viewed from the bottom, which we refer to as the bottom profile, to estimate the baseline. However, due to the presence of noise and attached artifacts, and shapes of characters such as H, F, and M which contribute many points that deviate significantly from the baseline, this set of points is heavily contaminated with outliers.

Among the various parameter estimation techniques, the RAndom Sample Consensus (RANSAC) algorithm (Fischler & Bolles, 1981) has been shown to perform robustly even in cases where the total population of data consists of up to 50% outliers. We therefore use RANSAC to estimate the baseline from the bottom profile of each word image. The cap line can be estimated in a similar manner from the top profile of every image, which is defined as the outer contour of characters as viewed from the top. A beneficial side effect of this procedure is that once the baseline and cap line are estimated, any artifacts that extend below or above these lines can be automatically eliminated in order to reduce the overall level of noise in the word image (if the extension in the bottom of the letter Q passes below the baseline in the font being used, the baseline will still be correctly estimated, but points below the baseline should not be eliminated). Furthermore, the average of the slopes of the baseline and the cap line can be used to correct slight orientation errors that may exist in a word image. Finally, the vertical distance between the two enclosing lines is used to compute the normalization factor and resize the word images to the target size. An example showing the different steps of this procedure can be found in Figure 4.

While the cap line is not defined for characters printed in lower case, the general procedure discussed above can still be used to normalize this type of text. However, this time we use the baseline and the mean line, which is an imaginary line that passes through the tops of characters such as "a" and "c", to normalize the word images. The estimation of the two enclosing lines is more difficult in this case compared to upper case characters since many more actual character segments, namely the ascenders (parts of characters such as "t" and "f" that rise above the mean line) and descenders (parts of characters such as "p" or "g" that extend below the baseline), contaminate the top and bottom profiles, respectively, and increase the ratio of outliers in the estimation data.

The majority of pixels in words printed in lower case can be considered to be located between the baseline and the mean line. We can therefore find this general area by computing the horizontal histogram of pixels in a word image, and eliminate most of the ascender and descender pixels by removing any rows in the image that contain less than 50% of the maximum count in the histogram. The baseline and the mean line will then be estimated from the top and bottom profiles of this new image, as shown in Figure 5. Similar to the procedure for capital letters, the average of the slopes of the two lines can be used to correct slight orientation errors that may exist in a word image.

4.4 Recognition engine

Hidden Markov models have had a long and successful history in the field of speech recognition. The similarity between many of the problems encountered in this field and those in text recognition has led to the widespread use of HMMs in both printed and handwritten character recognition, and in particular noisy, degraded, and/or connected text recognition (Bose & Kuo, 1994; Kim et al., 1997; Koerich et al., 2000; Likforman-Sulem & Sigelle, 2009; Schenkel & Jabri, 1998). The system described here also uses an HMM based classifier, and is most similar to the general structure of the HMM based recognition system proposed by Elms et al (Elms et al., 1998). However, the two systems are different in the type of

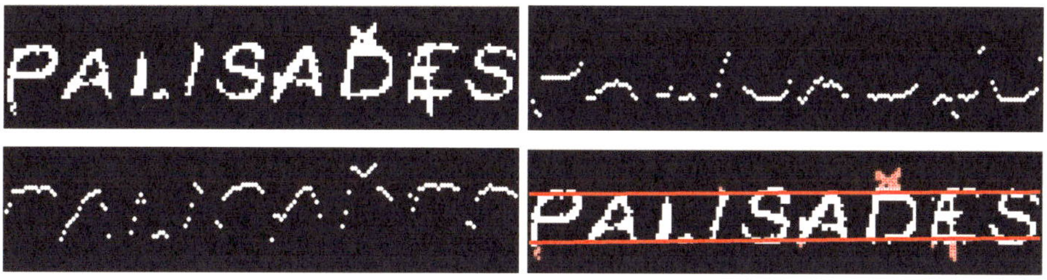

Fig. 4. Preprocessing using RANSAC for words printed in capital letters; Original image shown in the top left, top and bottom profiles shown in the top right and bottom left, and the fitted baseline, capline, and detected artifacts are shown in the bottom right

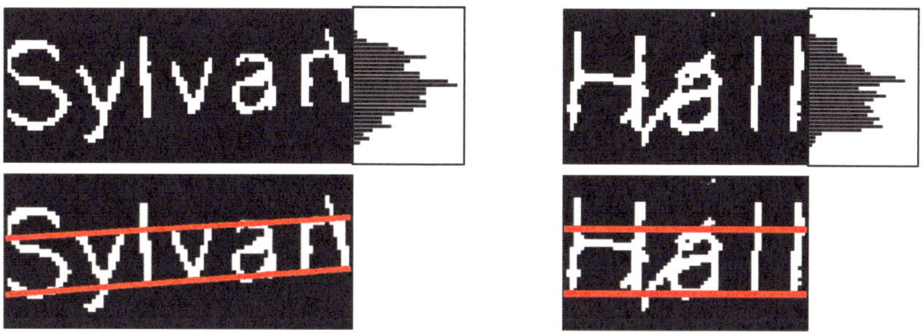

Fig. 5. Preprocessing using RANSAC for words printed in upper case and lower case; from top to bottom: Original word image and its corresponding horizontal histogram, Fitted baseline and mean line

feature vectors used for classification, clustering algorithm employed in the generation of codebooks, modeling of the white space in between characters, and the incorporation of letter transition probabilities into the Level Building Algorithm (LBA) (Rabiner & Levinson, 1985) that performs the implicit segmentation of word images into individual characters. Moreover, the system in (Elms et al., 1998) is trained on real character images and includes contextual knowledge in the form of a lexicon, whereas here we use artificial character images (as discussed in Section 4.2) for training and only use a simple language structure (letter transition probabilities) to improve the performance of our system. The different components of the proposed recognition engine are described next.

4.4.1 HMM structure & training

The full structure of a 2D image can only be properly captured if the relationships between the different points in both dimensions of the image are simultaneously captured. This method of feature extraction leads to the two dimensional (or planar) HMMs as seen in (Levin & Pieraccini, 1992), or the pseudo two dimensional HMMs in (Kuo & Agazzi, 1994). Alternatively, the information in each dimension can be modeled independently by separate HMMs so that simpler one dimensional HMMs can be employed. Here we have taken the latter approach, and use the consecutive rows and columns of normalized character images as features. Accordingly, two HMMs will be trained for each character class based on the quantized horizontal (row wise) or vertical (column wise) features extracted from images of characters in their corresponding classes. During recognition, the likelihood values for the horizontal and vertical HMMs will be combined based on the procedure explained in

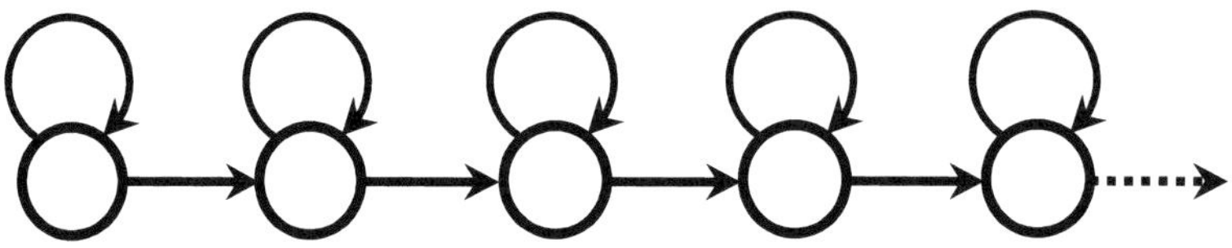

Fig. 6. Left to Right HMM with 5 states

Section 4.4.3. Quantization of the feature vectors is implemented according to two separate codebooks. The *K-means* algorithm is used to generate one codebook based on the horizontal feature vectors extracted from the training images belonging to every character class, and another one in a similar fashion from the vertical features (here we chose 45 cluster centers for both cases based on experimental results). All row wise and column wise features are then quantized using the nearest neighbor rule on their corresponding codebook.
We use the simple left-right structure shown in Figure 6 for each HMM. In this structure, transitions are restricted from a current state S_i only to the immediate next state S_{i+1} or back to itself so that each fixed number of observations will be generally modeled by one state. The total number of states is therefore directly dependent on the length of the observations and thereby the normalized size of the character images. Here we chose the parameters of the TDM to create artificial characters from the set A:Z using different fonts with a uniform height of 28 pixels, and centered each noisy character within a 38 by 38 pixel image (the padding on the sides of each character provides the necessary space for variations between width of characters such as "I" ad "W", and the linear artifacts generated by the EDM). The number of states for each HMM (horizontal and vertical) was then fixed at 10 states for every character class, so that there are approximately four observations per each state (in reality, some states may represent more or less number of observations depending on the particular character class and levels of noise and defects in the training images). It should also be noted that the prior state probability matrix of each HMM is normally estimated during training. However, the LBA requires the prior probability of the first state of every HMM to be equal to one (Rabiner & Levinson, 1985). Before training, the initial guess for the prior probabilities of the states of each HMM are therefore chosen according to this requirement. These settings will not be affected by the training procedure since parameters that are set to zero will remain unchanged.

4.4.2 Level building algorithm

As discussed in Section 4.2, segmentation of words extracted from maps using explicit methods is not a viable approach. The LBA provides a suitable alternative by simultaneously finding the jointly optimal segmentation and recognition results for each word image. The LBA is essentially an extension of the Viterbi algorithm. While an unknown sequence of observations extracted from a single character image can be matched against an HMM using the Viterbi algorithm, the LBA can use multiple HMMs to split an observation sequence extracted from a whole word image into subsequences and match them to individual models. Given a set of character models $\lambda = (\lambda^1, \lambda^2, \ldots, \lambda^N)$ and an observation sequence $O = (O^1, O^2, \ldots, O^T)$, the algorithm starts at level 1 by progressively scanning through O from left to right. The incremental likelihood of matching the partial sequence $(O^1, O^2, \ldots, O^t)$ to a model λ^n is then computed at each frame t and for every model, and stored in the array $P(1, t, n)$. At the end of level 1, the model that best describes the partial sequence $(O^1, O^2, \ldots, O^t)$ at each frame t and its corresponding likelihood are stored in the arrays $\hat{W}$

and $\hat{P}$:

$$\hat{W}(1,t) = \underset{n}{\text{argmax}} P(1,t,n) \tag{1}$$

$$\hat{P}(1,t) = \max_{n} P(1,t,n) \tag{2}$$

The computation at higher levels is carried out in a similar fashion, except that the cumulative likelihood for each model and at each frame t picks up from the best likelihood at frame $t-1$ in the previous level ($\hat{P}(l-1,t-1)$). In addition, a backpointer is maintained to keep track of the ending frame of the best previous model. This procedure is continued until a maximum number of levels l_{max} have been reached, at which point the algorithm backtracks from the best model at the last time frame T ($\hat{W}(l_{max},T)$) using the previously constructed backpointer array. The jointly optimal recognition and segmentation results are subsequently found from the sequence of best matching models and the backpointer array, respectively.

Horizontal features cannot be extracted from the word image unless the extents of its individual characters are known beforehand. We can therefore only use the vertical (column wise) features to construct an observation sequence for each word image. Accordingly, every word image is normalized in height such that it has a height of 28 pixels and centered within a 38 pixel high window (similar to the height format of the training images), while the width of each image is adjusted to maintain its aspect ratio. The column wise features are then quantized according to the codebook for vertical features obtained in training, and the LBA is applied to the resulting observation sequence based on the set of HMMs trained on vertical features. It should also be noted that in many cases the characters are separated by empty inter character space. A separate HMM is typically used to model this empty space (e.g. see (Elms et al., 1998)), in which case the maximum number of levels of the LBA needs to be increased to account for its occurrence. However, the training images used here already model this empty space by having extra padding to the sides. Since the extra empty space HMM is not needed here, we can use the width of each word image to hypothesize the maximum number of letters and thereby the maximum number of levels that need to be computed in the LBA as follows:

$$l_{max} = \lfloor T/\mu_{char} \rfloor + C \tag{3}$$

In this equation T is the total width of the word image (equivalent to its number of columns), μ_{char} is the mean character width found from the training images, and C is a constant which accounts for inter character blank spaces and the much smaller width of the letter "I" (here we set $C = 3$). Each normalized word image should therefore be processed by the LBA for levels 1 through l_{max}. The level l that generates the highest overall likelihood $\hat{P}(l,T)$ will then determine the optimal number of letters and the corresponding segmentation points for that word image.

In its current form, the LBA might match an unreasonably short or long sequence of observations to a single character model (for instance, the model for the character "A" may be matched against a sequence with 10 or 100 observations). Assuming that the width (or duration) of each character can be modeled by an individual Gaussian distribution, a temporal constraint can be included in the LBA by modifying the computation of the cumulative likelihoods $P(l,t,n)$ as follows (Rabiner & Levinson, 1985):

$$\tilde{P}(l,t,n) = P(l,t,n) \cdot P_n(d_{\Delta t})^{\alpha} \tag{4}$$

In this equation P_n is the Gaussian distribution for the width of character model λ^n with mean μ_n and variance σ_n, $d_{\Delta t}$ is the duration of the current observation subsequence being matched to model λ^n, and α is a weighting factor. The parameters for each individual Gaussian distribution (μ_n and σ_n) are obtained from the training images of their corresponding character model, and the value for α is optimized experimentally.
The absence of a syntax constraint in the LBA means that any character model is equally likely to follow another character model from a previous level. However, statistical analysis of the words in any given language shows that some pairs of characters are more likely to appear than others. For instance, in English the letter "Q" is always followed by the letter "U", and therefore the LBA should penalize the matching of letters other than "U" in the computation of cumulative likelihoods if the best character model at the previous level is a "Q". A bigram model specifies the probability with which a letter follows a previous letter in a word for a specific language. This simple statistical language model is consequently incorporated in the LBA using the following probability array in order to further improve its performance:

$$\check{P}_{n|m}(l-1,t-1) = \hat{P}(l-1,t-1) \cdot P_{tr}(n \mid m)^{\beta} \tag{5}$$

where n is the character corresponding to the current model λ^n being matched to a partial sequence of observations at level l, m is the best character from the previous level ($\hat{W}(l-1,t-1)$), $P_{tr}(n \mid m)$ is the appropriate letter transition probability, and β is weighting factor. At the beginning of each new level, $\check{P}_{n|m}(l-1,t-1)$ will thus substitute $\hat{P}(l-1,t-1)$ in the computation of cumulative likelihoods for each new character model λ^n to include the bigram model. Here we obtained the letter transition probabilities from Konheim (1981), and the value for β was optimized experimentally.

4.4.3 Combining classifiers

The segmented characters obtained from the LBA are processed by a separate classifier that also uses the horizontal HMMs for more robust recognition results. Each character is first normalized in size and centered within a 38 by 38 pixel image (similar to the training images) and its horizontal and vertical features are quantized according to their corresponding codebooks. Two arrays of likelihood values can now be computed for each character by matching the column wise and row wise observation sequences against all HMMs trained on vertical and horizontal features, respectively. A third array of likelihood values is obtained from evaluating the width of each character in the Gaussian width models of every character class. Assuming independence, these three arrays can then be combined into a single likelihood array through point-wise multiplication. However, the likelihood values from the character width models will be weighted similar to (4) using a factor α.
The arrays of likelihood values for each of the characters extracted from a word image can be assembled into a trellis where the number of nodes at each time step corresponds to the number of character classes and the number of time steps matches the total number of letters in that word (equal to the optimal number of levels in the LBA). At each time step (letter in the word), we then assign a score to the nth node (character class) that is equal to the value of the nth element in the combined likelihood array of the corresponding character image. The edges in the trellis represent a transition from a previous character class to the next one. We therefore associate a cost to each transition according the letter transition probabilities (the bigram model). Similar to (5), this cost will be weighted by a factor β.

Each path through this trellis represents a possible sequence of characters matching the word image, and the cost associated with its traversal can be computed based on the scores of the nodes and edges along the individual path. The optimal sequence of matching characters for each word image therefore corresponds to the best path through the trellis, which can be efficiently computed using the Viterbi algorithm.

5. Experimental results

Two experiments were performed to evaluate the effectiveness of the proposed text recognition system on street labels and place names extracted from several USGS topographic maps. In the first experiment, the character images for the training data were generated using the same fonts as the extracted text according to USGS style sheets. In the maps being tested here the street labels were printed in *Univers 53 Extended Oblique* (a sans serif font), whereas the place names used *Century Expanded* (a serif font). Both types of text were printed in all capital letters. In the second experiment, we used the generic fonts *Arial* (sans serif) and *Times New Roman* (serif) for the training data in order to assess the performance of the system in cases where the specific fonts used on the maps are not known. Both experiments were carried out according to the same procedure, and the implementation details that follow should be considered to apply to both cases.

5.1 Training

The artificial character images generated by the noise models described in Section 4.2 should closely mimic the defects and degradations seen in real characters extracted from maps. Correct estimation of the parameters that govern the behavior of these models is therefore critical to the overall performance of our recognition system.

Barney Smith (Smith, 2001) has proposed a method to estimate the blurring and threshold parameters from corners of characters in binarized scanned images, but the estimation of the remaining parameters in Baird's defect model is not discussed. Kanungo et al. (Kanungo et al., 2000) have developed a statistical bootstrapping method which tests the hypothesis that two sets of images belong to the same underlying distribution. Baird (Baird, 1999) showed that this method can be effectively used to make fine and accurate discriminations with regards to the parameters used in his character defect model.

Here we use a simple approach to find the suitable ranges of values for the parameters used in the TDM. Five samples of actual characters for each of the letters M, S, A, N, and R were first extracted from maps (a total of 25 samples). Each of the parameters in the TDM were then allowed to range within specific intervals, and a set of 60 artificial character images were rendered using each of the parameter settings. The Mean Square Error (MSE) of the images in each set of artificial characters with respect to the real character samples was subsequently computed, and averaged over the number of images in each set (60) and the total number of actual letter samples (25). A few combinations of parameter settings that produced the smallest MSEs were then selected to create the training images. Figure 7 shows samples of actual characters extracted from maps, and the artificial characters generated by the TDM and EDM using the above procedure.

For each character class A through Z and each font, 240 artificial characters were created using the TDM. The images for each character class were then combined such that characters from each font appeared in alternate positions in the training data. A second set of artificial characters were created and used as the input to the EDM (a grand total of $4 \times 26 \times 240 \approx$

Fig. 7. Samples of characters M and A when the fonts are known; First row are actual character samples from maps; second and third rows of images generated using the TDM and EDM, respectively

25000 character images). The HMMs were trained in two stages. First, the general structure of each character class was learned using only the images generated by the TDM. The noisier EDM images were then used to fine tune the parameters in each HMM.

5.2 Exception handling

Curvilinear text comprises only a very small percentage of the total amount of text in maps. Since individual characters in such words are situated along a curve (rather than a straight line), the preprocessing algorithm described in Section 4.3 cannot be used in such rare cases. As the LBA relies on proper normalization of the input words, a different character segmentation procedure should be used here.

During pyramid decomposition and the subsequent fitting of the individual word blobs with the minimum area enclosing rectangle (Section 4.1), curved words will show high variation in the distance between the bottom (or top) side of their enclosing rectangle and the bottom of the blob, whereas flat words will be snugly fit with the enclosing rectangle. Curved words can therefore be automatically identified.

The individual characters in curvilinear text are better separated from each other compared to regular text, which means they are better candidates for explicit segmentation algorithms. Here we used the algorithm in (Liang et al., 1994) to obtain the individual characters in such words. The combined classifier in Section 4.4.3 was subsequently utilized to recognize each word image.

5.3 Results

Table 1 summarizes the recognition results for the extracted street labels and place names using HMMs trained on actual and generic fonts (experiments I and II, respectively), and ABBYY FineReader 10 (a leading commercial OCR) which was used to benchmark our system. Here we used the single character edit distance which counts each insertion, deletion, and substitution as one error to compute the recognition rates. As expected, the commercial OCR performed well in cases where the level of noise and defects was low (e.g. the words "HIGHWOOD" and "LAFAYETTE" in Figure 2), but showed a drop in its recognition rate for words that were too noisy or not perfectly horizontal (e.g. the words "EDGEWATER", "MACKAY", and "AVE" in Figure 2). It should also be noted that both systems performed at close to 100% for the words printed in the serif font (*Century Expanded*). This could be an indication that serif fonts have more distinguishing features compared to the sans serif fonts.

Recognition Engine	Correct	Wrong	Recognition Rate
Experiment I (actual fonts)	964	63	93.87%
Experiment II (generic fonts)	936	91	91.14%
ABBYY FineReader10	921	106	89.68%

Table 1. Performance evaluation of recognition of characters: Our system vs. ABBYY FineReader10

6. Summary

In this chapter, we described a custom multi-font recognition system for text extracted from maps. The different components of this system have been designed to minimize the required amount of user involvement so that the overall cost of digitizing paper maps can be reduced. Using only artificially generated training data, this system was shown to produce acceptable recognition rates both when the actual fonts used for the text are known, and when only generic fonts are available. Since this system does not rely on prior knowledge in the form of gazetteers or lexicons, it can be easily configured to work with maps produced by different organizations and printed in languages other than English. However, if such information becomes available the existing system can be modified to take advantage of it using the Dictionary Viterbi Algorithm (Hull et al., 1983).

While the performance of the text extraction and recognition system described here is promising, the fully automatic conversion of paper maps into computer readable format remains an open problem due to the wide variability of the characteristics and features of maps produced by different organizations. As a result a realistic goal for any map conversion system should be to take advantage of user interaction when needed, but to limit the amount of user involvement to only a supervisory capacity.

The current recognition system can still be improved such that words that contain a mixture of both upper case and lower case characters, or letters and numbers can be processed at the same performance rate as words that contain only capital letters. A first step towards that direction would be to change the bigram probabilities so that they will allow transitions between lower case and upper case letters, and numbers, according to probability distributions learned from processing a large enough population of actual text samples extracted from maps.

7. References

Agazzi, O. E., Kuo, S., Levin, E. & Pieraccini, R. (1993). Connected and degraded text recognition using planar hidden Markov models, *Proceedings ICASSP'93*, pp. V113–V116.

Baird, H. S. (1992). Document image defect models, *in* H. S. Baird, H. Bunke & K. Yamamoto (eds), *Structured Document Image Analysis*, Springer, pp. 546–556.

Baird, H. S. (1999). Document image quality: Making fine discriminations, *In Proc. IAPR IntŠl Conf. on Document Analysis and Recognition*, pp. 459–462.

Baird, H. S. (2007). The state of the art of document image degradation modelling, *in* B. Chaudhuri (ed.), *Digital Document Processing: Major Directions and Recent Advances*, Springer, pp. 261–279.

Bose, C. B. & Kuo, S. S. (1994). Connected and degraded text recognition using hidden markov model, *Pattern Recognition* 27: 1345–1363.

Cao, R. & Tan, C. L. (2002). Text/graphics separation in maps, *GREC '01: Selected Papers from the Fourth International Workshop on Graphics Recognition Algorithms and Applications*, Springer-Verlag, London, UK, pp. 167–177.

Casey, R. G. & Lecolinet, E. (1996). A survey of methods and strategies in character segmentation, *IEEE Trans. Pattern Anal. Mach. Intell.* 18(7): 690–706.

Chen, L., Liao, H., Wang, J. & Fan, K. (1999). Automatic data capture for geographic information systems, *IEEE Trans. System, Man, and Cybernetics-part C: Applications and Reviews* 29(2): 205–215.

Chiang, Y., Knoblock, C. A. & Chen, C. (2005). Automatic extraction of road intersections from raster maps, *GIS '05: Proceedings of the 13th annual ACM international workshop on Geographic information systems*, pp. 267–276.

Dhar, D. B. & Chanda, B. (2006). Extraction and recognition of geographical features from paper maps, *Int. J. Doc. Anal. Recognit.* 8(4): 232–245.

Dori, D. & Wenyin, L. (1999). Automated CAD conversion with the machine drawing understanding system: Concepts, algorithms, and performance, *IEEE Trans. System, Man, and Cybernetics-part A: System and Humans* 29(4): 411–416.

Elms, A., Procter, S. & Illingworth, J. (1998). The advantage of using an HMM-based approach for faxed word recognition, *Int. J. Doc. Anal. Recognit.* 1(1): 18–36.

Fischler, M. A. & Bolles, R. C. (1981). Random sample consensus: a paradigm for model fitting with applications to image analysis and automated cartography, *Commun. ACM* 24(6): 381–395.

Gamba, P. & Mecocci, A. (1999). Perceptual grouping for symbol chain tracking in digitized topographic maps, *Pattern Recogn. Lett.* 20(4): 355–365.

Gelbukh, A. F., Levachkine, S. & Han, S.-Y. (2003). Resolving ambiguities in toponym recognition in cartographic maps, *GREC*, pp. 75–86.

Guillevic, D. & Suen, C. (1997). An HMM word recognition engine, *ICDAR'97*, IEEE Computer Society, pp. 544–547.

Hull, J. (1998). Document image skew detection: Survey and annotated bibliography, *in* J. Hull & S. Taylor (eds), *Document Analysis Systems II*, World Scientific, pp. 40–64.

Hull, J., Srihari, S. & Choudhari, R. (1983). An integrated algorithm for text recognition: Comparison with a cascaded algorithm, *IEEE Trans. Pattern Anal. Mach. Intell.* 5(4): 384–395.

Kanungo, T., Haralick, R. M., Baird, H. S., Stuezle, W. & Madigan, D. (2000). A statistical, nonparametric methodology for document degradation model validation, *IEEE Transactions on Pattern Analysis and Machine Intelligence* 22: 1209–1223.

Kerle, N. & Leeuw, J. (2009). Reviving legacy population maps with object-oriented image processing techniques, *IEEE Transactions on Geoscience and Remote Sensing* 47(7): 2392–2402.

Khotanzad, A. & Zink, E. (2003). Contour line and geographic feature extraction from USGS color topographical paper maps, *IEEE Trans. Pattern Anal. Mach. Intell.* 25(1): 18–31.

Kim, H., Kim, S., Kim, K. & Lee, J. (1997). An HMM-based character-recognition network using level building, *Pattern Recognition* 30(3): 491–502.

Koerich, A., Koerich, R. L., Sabourin, R., El-Yacoubi, A. & Suen, C. Y. (2000). A syntax-directed level building algorithm for large vocabulary handwritten word recognition, *In Proc. 4th International Workshop on Document Analysis Systems*, pp. 255–266.

Konheim, A. G. (1981). *Cryptography: A Primer*, Wiley, New York, pp. 24–25.

Kuo, S. S. & Agazzi, O. E. (1994). Keyword spotting in poorly printed documents using pseudo 2-d hidden Markov models, *IEEE Trans. Pattern Anal. Mach. Intell.* 16(8): 842–848.

Levachkine, S., Velázquez, A., Alexandrov, V. & Kharinov, M. (2002). Semantic analysis and recognition of raster-scanned color cartographic images, *GREC '01: Selected Papers from the Fourth International Workshop on Graphics Recognition Algorithms and Applications*, pp. 178–189.

Levin, E. & Pieraccini, R. (1992). Dynamic planar warping for optical character recognition, *Proceedings ICASSP'92*, pp. III 149–III 152.

Leyk, S., Boesch, R. & Weibel, R. (2006). Saliency and semantic processing: Extracting forest cover from historical topographic maps, *Pattern Recogn.* 39(5): 953–968.

Li, L., Nagy, G., Samal, A., Seth, S. C. & Xu, Y. (2000). Integrated text and line-art extraction from a topographic map, *Int. J. of Doc. Anal. Recognit.* 2(4): 177–185.

Liang, S., Sridhar, M. & Ahmadi, M. (1994). Segmentation of touching characters in printed document recognition, *Pattern Recognition* 27(6): 825–840.

Likforman-Sulem, L. & Sigelle, M. (2009). Combination of dynamic bayesian network classifiers for the recognition of degraded characters, *SPIE Document Recognition and Retrieval XVI*, pp. 1–10.

Lu, Z. (1998). Detection of text regions from digital engineering drawings, *IEEE Trans. Pattern Anal. Mach. Intell.* 20(4): 431–439.

Namane, A., Soubari, E., Djebari, A., Meyruels, P. & Bruynooghe, M. (2006). Hopfield-multilayer-perceptron serial combination for accurate degraded printed character recognition, *Optical Engineering* 45(8): 087201.1–087201.15.

Pezeshk, A. & Tutwiler, R. L. (2008a). Contour line recognition and extraction from scanned color maps using dual quantization of the intensity image, *IEEE Southwest Symposium on Image Analysis and Interpretation*, pp. 173–176.

Pezeshk, A. & Tutwiler, R. L. (2008b). Text segmentation and reorientation from scanned color topographic maps, *10th IASTED Intl. Conference on Signal and Image Processing*, pp. 94–97.

Pezeshk, A. & Tutwiler, R. L. (2010a). Extended character defect model for recognition of text from maps, *IEEE Southwest Symposium on Image Analysis and Interpretation*, pp. 85–88.

Pezeshk, A. & Tutwiler, R. L. (2010b). Improved Multi Angled Parallelism for separation of text from intersecting linear features in scanned topographic maps, *ICASSP 2010*, pp. 1078–1081.

Pouderoux, J., Gonzato, J.-C., Pereira, A. & Guitton, P. (2007). Toponym recognition in scanned color topographic maps, *ICDAR '07: Proceedings of the Ninth International Conference on Document Analysis and Recognition*, pp. 531–535.

Rabiner, L. R. & Levinson, S. E. (1985). A speaker-independent, syntax-directed, connected word recognition system based on hidden Markov models and level building, *IEEE Trans. Acoustics, Speech, and Signal Processing* ASSP-33(3): 561–573.

Roy, P. P., Llados, J. & Pal, U. (2007). Text/graphics separation in color maps, *ICCTA '07: Proceedings of the International Conference on Computing: Theory and Applications*, pp. 545–551.

Sarfraz, M., Zidouri, A. & Shahab, S. (2005). A novel approach for skew detection of document images in OCR system, *CGIV'05*, IEEE Computer Society, pp. 175–180.

Schenkel, M. & Jabri, M. (1998). Low resolution, degraded document recognition using neural networks and hidden Markov models, *Pattern Recognition Letters* 19(3-4): 365–371.

Smith, E. H. B. (2001). Estimating scanning characteristics from corners, *In Proc. SPIE Document Recognition and Retrieval VIII, Volume 4307*, pp. 176–183.

Tombre, K., Tabbone, S., Pélissier, L., Lamiroy, B. & Dosch, P. (2002). Text/graphics separation revisited, *in: Workshop on Document Analysis Systems (DAS)*, Springer-Verlag, pp. 200–211.

Velázquez, A. & Levachkine, S. (2003). Text/graphics separation and recognition in raster-scanned color cartographic maps, *the Fifth International Workshop on Graphics Recognition Algorithms and Applications(GREC2001)*, pp. 63–74.

Wenyin, L., Zhang, W. & Yan, L. (2007). An interactive example-driven approach to graphics recognition in engineering drawings, *Int. J. Doc. Anal. Recognit.* 9(1): 13–29.

5

Grid'5000 Based Large Scale OCR Using the DTW Algorithm: Case of the Arabic Cursive Writing

Mohamed Labidi[1], Maher Khemakhem[2] and Mohamed Jemni[3]
[1]*Research Unit UTIC, ESSTT/ University of Tunis, Tunis*
[2]*MIRACL Lab, FSEGS/ University of Sfax, Sfax*
[3]*Research Unit UTIC, ESSTT/ University of Tunis, Tunis*
Tunisia

1. Introduction

Large scale optical character recognition (OCR) refers to or means the computerization of large amounts of documents such as news papers. Despite the diversity of commercial OCR products, this task still remains too far from the mature especially if the input documents are insufficient quality or cursive writing such as the Arabic documents (Vinciarelli, 2002). Indeed, in their project (Holley, 2009), the national library of Australia reports that existing OCR systems are, commonly, weak. Moreover, their conducted experiments on historical newspapers show that the corresponding accuracy raw varied from 71% to 98.02%. This is surely due to the weakness of the approaches and techniques used in these systems.
Printed cursive written documents such as the Arabic one presents, in addition, other difficulties which are behind the weaknesses of the existing commercialized systems especially when the quality of the input binary image of the document is not good enough. The first difficulty encountered for such writing is the segmentation of any given input word or sub-word into isolated characters given that the size of each of which is variable. In practice, if the segmentation process is conducted successfully, then it eases the recognition step to a large extent. That is why Latin printed OCR systems are, commonly, more powerful compared to those devoted to the cursive writing documents.
Dynamic Time Warp (DTW) algorithm is a well known procedure especially in pattern recognition (Alves et al., 2002; Khemakhem et al., 2005; Philip, 1992; Vuori et al., 2001), (Khemakhem et al., 2009; Kumar et al., 2006; Tapia et al., 2007). The DTW algorithm is the result of the adaptation of dynamic programming to the field of pattern recognition. Printed cursive writing OCR by the DTW algorithm provides very interesting recognition rates without prior character segmentation (such as: the Arabic, Persian, Urdu, latin connected characters,...), (Khemakhem et al., 2005). The purpose of the DTW algorithm is to perform optimal time alignment between a reference pattern and an unknown pattern and evaluate their difference. Intensive experiments show that the recognition rate of the DTW algorithm remains acceptable compared to the existing commercialized systems even when the quality of the input documents is not good enough. Intensive tests on more than 100.000 connected characters (most of them are Arabic cursive and including some important noise) show that the segmentation average rate is greater than 98% and the recognition average rate is

greater than 97% (Abedi et al., 2004). Consequently, we think that it is possible to build a powerful OCR system based on the DTW algorithm. Unfortunately, the enormous amount of computing to be achieved constitutes, however, the main drawback and hence restricts the use of the DTW algorithm.

Several works and approaches have been proposed to solve this problem (Philip, 1992) (Alves et al., 2002; Khemakhem et al., 2007; 2005; 1993). We are rather interested in this paper in the distributed systems and their possibilities to provide, costless and on demand, enough computing power which can ensure the substantial reduction of the DTW response time. Indeed, we found in our previous work that the response time of this algorithm is proportional to the provided computing power (Khemakhem et al., 2009). This quite means that if we own a grid computing then we can reach very interesting and increasing speedup factors.

Grid computing is an attractive infrastructure that provides a huge computing power, (Buyya et al., 2005; Foster et al., 2002; IBM, 2003; Khemakhem et al., 2009) without any prior investment. This is due to its ability to interconnect many computer networks of several organizations at the same time. Consequently, users can share many heterogeneous computer resources such us computing power. In our previous work, we have shown through an analytical and experimental studies (Khemakhem et al., 2009), that grid infrastructures can provide an adequate solution to very large quantities of Arabic documents OCR. Unfortunately, in our previous work we did not find the opportunity to make experiments on a scalable grid where we can achieve more significant experimental performance evaluation. Recently and fortunately the occasion has been provided to us to make intensive experiments on the French Grid'5000. Consequently, we report in this chapter these results which confirm, indeed, the results of our previous works.

This chapter starts with a brief presentation of the state of the art in terms of large scale OCR systems. Then, it presents and formulates the printed cursive Writing OCR by the DTW algorithm. In the forth part, a brief overview on grid computing and Grid'5000 platform are stated. The fifth part details the experimental conditions and the performance evaluation. Finally, we conclude and present some perspectives of this work.

2. Related work

A few solutions for large scale OCR are provided by computer scientists. Representative examples including OCRGrid (Goto, 2006), OCRopus (http://www.ocropus.org), Kirtas(http://www.kirtas.com) and The Australian Newspaper Digitization Project (Holley, 2009).

OCRGrid is a platform for distributed and cooperative OCR systems. The main idea of OCRGrid consists of deploying a lot of OCR servers on a network to allow end users to search for and use the adequate server. As servers can cooperate with each other, clients can benefit from a distributed parallel environment and consequently accelerate OCR tasks. On the other hand, applications searching for improving accuracy can benefit from OCRGrid due to the use of Majority logic technique which requires the running of many OCR engines. A multilingual processing environment can be also realized by combining a lot of community-supported OCR servers for various languages with localized dictionaries.

OCRopus is an open source OCR system sponsored by Google. It targets with its service the research community by improving the state of the art in optical character recognition and sought to serve also the large scale commercial document conversions. The system applications include modern digital library and the recognition of classical literature. Its main perspective consists of familiarizing the system with more languages so as to become omni-lingual and omni-script through contributing in open source community. Although the system has been evolving, it has not yet incorporated the Arabic language into its framework. Kirtas technology is an automatic book scanner which can do batch OCR for large volumes of books and other documents. By using innovative "automatic page-turning scanner" technology and a high-resolution Canon digital camera, Kirtas ensures image processing, quality control, OCR and Metadata. It can handle 15 left-to-right languages including English and French, 5 right-to-left languages including Arabic and 3 bilingual languages including Arabic/English. Kirtas OCR processing rates are too fast (about 1 page per second). Many public and university libraries decided to exploit Kirtas technology to digitize their old books. For all this, such a technology is too expensive and only rich institutions can afford to implement it.

National library of Australia has used OCR software to establish a large scale Historic Digitization Project. The Australian Newspaper Digitization Program (ANDP) claimed that 'acceptable' OCR was still to be improved. Besides, the poor quality of the original source documents urged the National Library of Australia to work with what was at hand but to anticipate the lack of OCR accuracy. In order to improve the quality of OCR accuracy, the committee of the Library adopted from the thirteen methods they came out with only five new ones, which are going to be tested and investigated. These methods are mostly to compare image optimization software, to experiment using greyscale files, to use Australian dictionaries, to clean/correct OCR text manually, and to use confusion matrix and language modeling post/during OCR processing. They searched for improving OCR accuracy by using both a combination of methods and manual methods of humans correcting the mistakes of machines. The Australian library was considered leading in that it was the first worldwide to involve public users in the correction of texts instead of the contractor. Such a solution was considered labor intensive for the Library before the emergence of web 2.0 technologies. Although the public was not informed that they could introduce any corrections to the texts, they embarked on this correction immediately. There were measures decided to check the accuracy of the OCR-corrected text via counting the number of lines corrected and number of different articles corrected. However, the interventions of public users may badly affect the content of the articles so they thought of monitoring and moderation to make sure that no data has been added to the original text.

In the next section, we will present the basics of the DTW algorithm which is considered the corner stone of our proposal to solve the problem of large scale OCR.

3. The DTW algorithm

This algorithm is a well known procedure especially in pattern recognition (Philip, 1992) (Alves et al., 2002; Khemakhem et al., 2007; Tapia et al., 2007; Vinciarelli, 2002; Vuori et al., 2001). The purpose of this procedure is to perform an optimal time alignment between a reference pattern and an unknown pattern and evaluate their difference. What makes the DTW procedure very attractive is its ability to recognize properly cursive characters (connected blocks of characters such as words or parts of words in Arabic) without need of a prior segmentation into characters according to a given reference library of isolated characters. The adaptation of this procedure to the Arabic cursive OCR has shown to provide very interesting results (Khemakhem et al., 2007; 2005).

3.1 Cursive writing OCR by the DTW algorithm

Words in any cursive writing, such as the Arabic language, are inherently written in blocks of connected characters. While the segmentation of the text into blocks of connected characters is a preliminary phase to the recognition process, a further segmentation of these blocks into separate characters is usually adopted. Indeed, many researchers have considered the segmentation of Arabic words into isolated characters before performing the recognition phase (AlBadr et al., 1998; Cheung et al., 2001; Vuori et al., 2001). The crux of the viability of the use of DTW technique is then its ability and efficiency to perform the recognition without the prior segmentation of blocks into separate characters.

Let V represents a reference library of$R$ trained characters $Cr, r = 1, 2, , R$. defining the Arabic alphabet in some given fonts. We here stress the fact that several fonts could be considered even simultaneously It suffices to get them trained which is easily done at the learning phase while constructing the reference library V. Let T represents a block of connected Arabic characters to be recognized. T is then composed of a sequence of N feature vectors Ti that are actually representing the concatenation of some subsequences of feature vectors representing each an unknown character to be recognized. The text T is seen as lying on the time axis (the X-axis) in such a manner that feature vector Ti stands at time i on this axis. The reference library V is portrayed on the Y-axis, where the reference character Cr is of length $lr, 1 \leq r \leq R$. According to (Khemakhem et al., 2007). Let $S(i, j, r)$ represents the cumulative distance at point (i, j) relative to the reference character Cr. The objective is then to detect simultaneously and dynamically the number of characters making T and recognizing these characters. There exists surely a number k and indices $(m1, m2, ..., mk)$ such that $Cm1 + Cm2 + ... + Cmk$ represents the optimal alignment to text T where denotes the concatenation operation. The path warping from point $(1, 1, m1)$ to point (N, lmk, k) and representing the optimal alignment is therefore of minimum cumulative distance that is:

$$S(N, l_{m_k}, k) = \min_{1 \leq r \leq R} \{S(N, l_r, r)\} \tag{1}$$

This path, however, is not continuous since it spans many different characters. We therefore must allow at any time the transition from the end of one reference character to the beginning of a new character. The end of reference character C_r is first reached whenever the warping function reaches the point (i, l_r, r) where $i = \lceil \frac{l_r+1}{2} \rceil, ..., N$. The warping function always reaches the ends of the reference characters. At each time i, we allow the start of the warping function at the beginning of each reference character along with the addition of the smallest cumulative distance among the end points found at time $(i - 1)$. The resulting functional equations are:

$$S(i, j, r) = D(i, j, r) + \min_{\substack{1 \leq i \leq N \\ 1 \leq j \leq l_r \\ 1 \leq r \leq R}} \left\{ \begin{array}{c} S(i-1, j, r), \\ S(i-1, j-1, r), \\ S(i-1, j-2, r) \end{array} \right\} \tag{2}$$

with the boundary conditions :

$$S(i,1,r) = D(i,1,r) + \min_{\substack{1+\lceil \frac{1+\min_{1\le r\le R}\{l_r\}}{2} \rceil \le i \le N \\ 1 \le k \le R \\ 1 \le r \le R}} S(i-1, l_k, k) \quad (3)$$

To trace back the warping function and the optimal alignment path, we have to memorize the transition time from one reference character to the others (Khemakhem et al., 2007). This can easily be accomplished by the following procedure:

$$b(i,j,r) = trace \min_{\substack{1 \le i \le N \\ 1 \le j \le l_r \\ 1 \le r \le R}} \left\{ \begin{array}{c} b(i-1,j,r), \\ b(i-1,j-1,r), \\ b(i-1,j-2,r) \end{array} \right\} \quad (4)$$

Where *trace* min is a function that returns the element corresponding to the term that minimizes the functional equations.

4. Grid computing

A grid is a collection of machines, sometimes referred to as nodes, resources, members, donors, clients, hosts, engines, and many other such terms. They all contribute any combination of resources to the grid as a whole. Some resources may be used by all users of the grid while others may have specific restrictions, (Bahi et al., 2006; Buyya et al., 2005; Foster et al., 2002; IBM, 2003; Shi et al., 2006).
In most organizations, there are large amounts of under utilized computing resources. Most desktop machines are busy less than 5 percent of the time. In some organizations, even the server machines can often be relatively idle. Grid computing provides a framework for exploiting these under utilized resources and thus has the possibility of substantially increasing the efficiency of resource usage (IBM, 2003).
Often, machines may have enormous unused disk drive capacity. Grid computing, more specifically, a data grid, can be used to aggregate this unused storage into a much larger virtual data store, possibly configured to achieve improved performance and reliability over that of any single machine (IBM, 2003).
Consequently, a grid computing is an infrastructure that allows to many institutions (regardless their geographical locations) to interconnect a large collection of their heterogeneous computer networks and systems to share together a set of software and/or hardware resources, services, licences ... (Buyya et al., 2005; Foster et al., 2002; IBM, 2003). This huge ability of sharing resources in various combinations will lead to many advantages such as: *Increase the efficiency of resource usage;
*Facilitate the remote collaboration between: institutions, researchers, ...
*Give to users a huge computing power;
*Give to users a huge storage capacity, etc.
Some researchers attempt now to model and realize this infrastructure in the right manner and some others attempt to anticipate and to take the expected advantages of such infrastructure

to solve several problems, (Bahi et al., 2006; Buyya et al., 2005; Foster et al., 2002; IBM, 2003; Shi et al., 2006).

4.1 Grid'5000

Grid'5000 is a French research effort developing a large scale nation wide infrastructure for Grid research. 17 French laboratories are involved, nation wide, in the objective of providing the community of Grid researchers a test bed allowing experiments in all the software layers between the network protocols up to the applications (Bolze et al., 2006). The Grid'5000 platform is intended to support research in all areas of computer science related to large scale distributed processing and networking. Researchers should use Grid'5000 in the perspective of large scale experiments (at least 3 sites and 1000 CPUs). They may generate useful results for other communities, as long as the community of computer science researchers learns something from Grid'5000 experiments. It is a shared tool, used by many people with different and varying needs. The administrators pursue the following objectives, the main one being the first of this list:

1.Make the tool available to experiments involving a significant number of nodes (in the 1000's). To make this possible, reservation fragmentation must be avoided as much as possible.

2.Keep the platform available for the development of experiments during the day. Therefore, reservations using all the nodes available on one site during work hours (in France) should be avoided in general.

Amongst the advantages of this grid is the ease of its reconfiguration. Indeed, whenever a user wants to perform experiments on Grid'5000, he has to make a prior reservation of a fixed number of nodes for a precise duration of time. Once the request of this user is accepted, he will be the lone authorized to exploit reserved nodes during the required period. A minimal set of software is installed on the nodes of each site. Sometimes a user should create a "Kadeploy" [1] image in which other software package that he needs can be included. He should also deploy it on the authorized nodes before its utilization.

The aim of this chapter is to prove trough intensive experiments over Grid'5000 that such infrastructure constitutes maybe the only way to solve the problem of costless computerization of big quantities of cursive writing documents using the DTW algorithm.

4.2 Deployment of the Arabic OCR over the Grid'5000

Recall that the objective of the present chapter is to validate the analytical results found in our previous work which reveal that grid computing is an adequate infrastructure to build a powerful distributed system which is able to perform large scale OCR, (Khemakhem et al., 2009).

It is commonly known that if we would like to distribute any given application over any given distributed infrastructure, one could make a decision about the adequate way to achieve it. Indeed, we can exploit either the inherent parallelism of the application algorithms or the corresponding data distribution or maybe both. For our application, we found in our previous work (Khemakhem et al., 1993) that the only way to reach interesting and customized speedup for the recognition process of the Arabic OCR based on the DTW algorithm is to proceed to

[1] Kadeploy is a fast and scalable deployment system towards cluster and grid computing. It provides a set of tools, for cloning, configuring (post installation) and managing a set of nodes. Currently it deploys successfully linux, *BSD, Windows, Solaris on x86 and 64 bits computers.

the data distribution. It means that we have to assign to each processor participating in the work, both, the application executable and a part of the data to be processed. Such solution is simpler and induces a very large degree of distribution. Our strategy consists of using one node of the grid as master and the remaining nodes as workers. During our experiments, each worker has been assigned by the same number of binary images which represents a part of the overall documents to be processed because all of the used grid workers are homogeneous (see table 1). For each experiment, the number of binary images to be assigned to each worker is calculated according to the number of workers participating in the work. The master starts by assigning to each worker the Arabic OCR Application and a part of the input documents to be computerized (in the form of binary image files). Next, it launches remotely the recognition process on each worker. For each input binary image file the target worker generates an output ascii file giving the recognition result. these files are turned back to the master.

5. Performance evaluation of massive cursive writing OCR over the GRID'5000

To ascertain our thesis which considers that grid infrastructures constitute an adequate solution (and maybe the only way) to solve the problem of large scale Arabic OCR without any prior investment, we have conducted intensive experiments over the grid'5000. These experiments have concerned the distribution of a corpus test composed of 10000 binary image files. Each image contains around 1200 characters.
Recall that the principle of our deployment consists to take the input binary images of the arabic documents to be processed (each image corresponds to a single document page) and then assign them optimally or pseudo optimally among the targeted computers (denoted by workers) of the grid. This means that every computer participating in the work will be assigned, naturally, according to its own computing power.

5.1 The experimental conditions

Cluster	Location	Cluster type	Nodes	CPU Type	Frequency	Memory
Capricorne	Lyon	IBM eServer 326	56	AMD Opteron 246	2.0GHz	2 GB
Sagittaire	Lyon	Sun Fire V20z	79	AMD Opteron 250	2.4GHz	2GB
Gdx	Orsay	IBM eServer 326m	312	AMD Opteron 246	2.0 GHz	2 GB
Netgdx	Orsay	IBM eServer 326m	30	AMD Opteron 246	2.0 GHz	2 GB

Table 1. Hardware configuration of the Grid testbed

Experiments were conducted using 4 clusters of 2 different sites in France. The hardware configuration is shown in table 1. Debian GNU/Linux 4.0 is the operating system of all used workers. For the software, we used specialized scripts shell to assign tasks and keep the recognition results. As described at the Section 4.1, the nodes must be reconfigured at each utilization.

5.2 Results and performance evaluation

5.2.1 The studied corpus

We have used a corpus of 10000 images which have been assigned optimally and pseudo optimally among the authorized workers. Figure 1 illustrates a sample of the studied corpus.

أثناء حراسة الأماكن العامة، عندما يقابل هذا الروبوت الشخص
المشتبه به، وجها لوجه، يلتقط لهذا الأخير صورة ثم يرسلها
لاسلكيا الى مركز العمليات التابع لجهاز الشرطة المحلي الذي
يرسل على الفور دورية للقبض على المشتبه به والتحقيق معه.

وتأمل شركة "ألسوك" في استعمال هذا الروبوت في جميع
الأماكن العامة، الواقعة في محيط عملها الأمني، فضلا عن
استخدامه في المطارات ومحطات القطارات لمكافحة الإرهاب

أثناء حراسة الأماكن العامة، عندما يقابل هذا الروبوت الشخص
المشتبه به، وجها لوجه، يلتقط لهذا الأخير صورة ثم يرسلها
لاسلكيا الى مركز العمليات التابع لجهاز الشرطة المحلي الذي
يرسل على الفور دورية للقبض على المشتبه به والتحقيق معه.

وخرج من بيته أول النهار فلقيه بعض الفقراء فقال له يا
سيدي أريد ان تعطنى القصيدة التي مدحت بها
قال اى قصيدة تريد فقال التي أولها أمن تذكر جيران الخ
فاعطاها له وجرى ذكرها في الناس ولما بلغت الصاحب
بهاء الدين وزير الملك الظاهر استنسخها

أثناء حراسة الأماكن العامة، عندما يقابل هذا الروبوت الشخص
المشتبه به، وجها لوجه، يلتقط لهذا الأخير صورة ثم يرسلها
لاسلكيا الى مركز العمليات التابع لجهاز الشرطة المحلي الذي
يرسل على الفور دورية للقبض على المشتبه به والتحقيق معه.

وتأمل شركة "ألسوك" في استعمال هذا الروبوت في جميع
الأماكن العامة، الواقعة في محيط عملها الأمني، فضلا عن
استخدامه في المطارات ومحطات القطارات لمكافحة الإرهاب

أثناء حراسة الأماكن العامة، عندما يقابل هذا الروبوت الشخص
المشتبه به، وجها لوجه، يلتقط لهذا الأخير صورة ثم يرسلها
لاسلكيا الى مركز العمليات التابع لجهاز الشرطة المحلي الذي
يرسل على الفور دورية للقبض على المشتبه به والتحقيق معه.

Fig. 1. A sample of the studied corpus

5.2.2 Results found

In this section we present the obtained results of the studied application over the Grid'5000. Indeed, the next results cover the distribution of the already presented corpus over a variable number of homogeneous nodes of Grid'5000 varying from 39 to 426.

Figure 2 illustrates the recognition time against the number of workers used. The horizontal axis represents the number of used workers and the vertical axis shows the corresponding recognition time. We observe that the recognition time decreases significantly with the increase of the number of workers. Indeed, we show that the time required to recognize the totality of the studied corpus decreases from 334 minutes by using 39 workers to 35 minutes by using 426 workers. Recall that the recognition of the corpus in the sequential mode requires approximately 10797 minutes which is equivalent to more than one week! such results confirm that the response time of the recognition process is proportional to the provided computing power, (Khemakhem et al., 2009). Consequently, we can confirm that grid infrastructure is adequate to solve the large scale OCR problem such as the computerization of library of books by using the DTW algorithm which is almost impossible to perform sequentially.
Figure 3 illustrates the speedup of the described experiment against the number of workers used. The horizontal axis represents the number of workers used and the vertical axis gives the speedup factor. We observe that the speedup is an increasing function of the

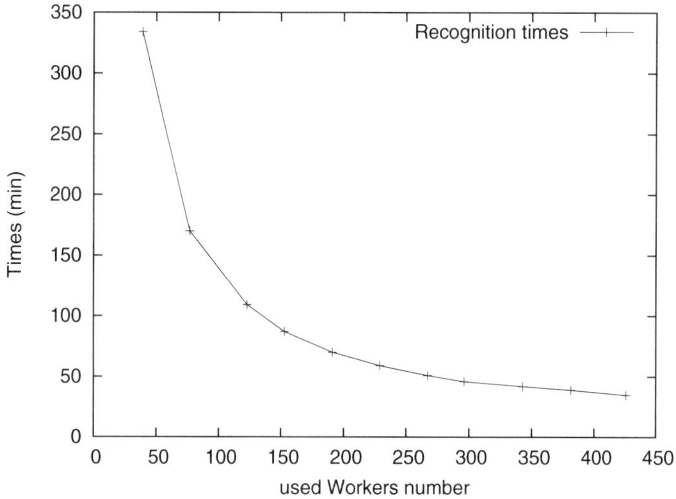

Fig. 2. The total recognition time of the studied corpus

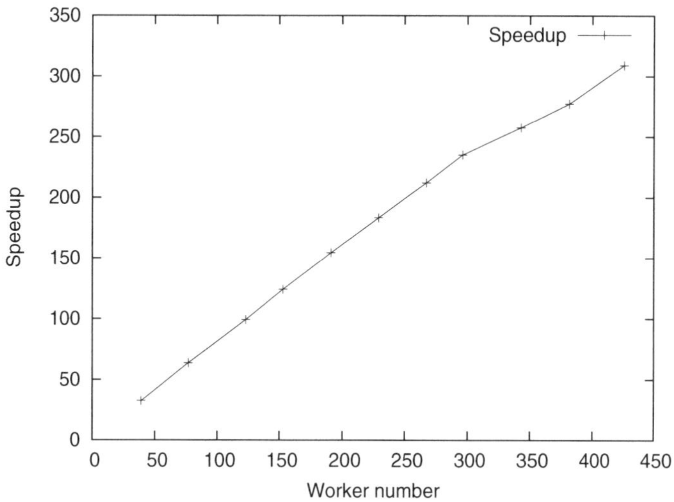

Fig. 3. Speedup factor

used workers. This figure shows, indeed, that we can reach interesting speedup factors; for example by using 426 workers, we reached 309 as speedup factor. This means that our proposed distributed system is able to recognize more than 5500 characters a second. We note that our sequential system is able to recognize only 18 characters a second. Such results confirm that grid'5000 is an adequate infrastructure to speedup drastically the response time of the DTW algorithm. Furthermore, with such enough computing power, we can improve the recognition rate by adding some complementary approaches and techniques. As a way to reach this expectation, we can use, for example, rich lexicons where we can check all recognized words and sub words and try to overcome those which don't have any linguistic meaning. Besides, we are convinced that volunteer grids (Khemakhem et al., 2009) can be considered also as amongst the adequate infrastructures which can solve large scale OCR given that the corresponding resources (workers) aren't condemned like those of dedicated grids. That is why the experimental study of these infrastructures presents for us also another perspective despite the corresponding challenges especially the volatility of nodes participating in the work and the security of data to be processed. Consequently we are faced to two issues: the fault tolerance and the data integrity (such as data alteration) problems. To solve these problems, the use of middleware seems to be mandatory to deploy efficiently large scale cursive writing OCR over volunteer grids.

6. Conclusion and perspectives

In this chapter we have shown how grid environments are able to solve both problems; the large scale OCR and the complex computing power of the DTW algorithm. The enough computing and storage power provided by any grid environment make very attractive our proposal. Indeed, these can help a lot to consider other types of complementary post treatment approaches and techniques to the DTW algorithm which will lead, surely, to the improvement of its recognition rate. Several investigations are under study especially the selection and then the integration of some other complementary approaches and/or techniques which can enhance the recognition rate of our proposal. In addition, the use of an appropriate middleware to manage data scheduling and ensure the fault tolerance seems to be mandatory if we wish to migrate to volunteer grid.

7. Acknowledgment

Experiments presented in this chapter were carried out using the Grid'5000 experimental testbed, being developed under the INRIA ALADDIN development action with support from CNRS, RENATER and several Universities as well as other funding bodies (see https://www.grid5000.fr).

8. References

Abedi, N. et Khemakhem, M.(2004) Reconnaissance de Caractères Imprimés Cursifs Arabes Par Comparaison Dynamique et Modèles Cachés de Markov, *in Proceedings of GEI Tunisia*, pp. 56-63, Monastir, Tunisia, March 2004.

AlBadr, A.& Haralick, R.(1998). A segmentation free approach to text recognition with application to Arabic text, *International Journal On Document Analysis And Recognition (IJDAR)*,, Vol. 1, No. 3, pp.147-166, 1998.

Alves, C, E, R. Caceres, E, N.& Dehne,F.(2002). Parallel Dynamic Programming for solving the String Editing Problem *Proceedings of the fourteenth annual ACM symposium on Parallel algorithms and architectures*, ISBN:1-58113-529-7, Winnipeg, Manitoba, Canada, August 10-13, 2002.

Bahi, J, M. Couturier, R. Mazouzi, K.& Salomo, M. (2006) Synchronous and asynchronous solution of a 3D transport model in a grid computing environment, *Applied Mathematical Modelling*,, Vol. 30, pp. 616-628 2006

Bolze, R.& all. (2006). Grid'5000: a large scale and highly reconfigurable grid experimental testbed, *International Journal of High Performance Computing Applications*,, Vol. 20, No. 4, pp. 481-494 Winter 2006.

Buyya, R.& Venugopal, S. (2005). A Gentle introduction to Grid Computing and Technologies, *CSI Communications*, Vol. 29, No. 1, pp.9-19, India, May 7-19, 2005.

Cheung, A. Bennamoun, M.& Bergman, N. (2001). An Arabic optical character recognition system using recognition based segmentation, *Pattern Recongnition,*, pp. 215-233, 2001.

Foster, I. Kesselman, C. & Tuecke, S.(2002). The Anatomy of the Grid, *Intl J. Supercomputer Applications*, Vol. 15, (2001) pp.200-222.

Goto, H. (2006). OCRGrid: A Platform for Distributed and Cooperative OCR Systems, *18th International Conference on Pattern Recognition (ICPR'06)*, Vol. 2, pp.982-985, 2006

Holley, R. (2009). How Good Can It Get? Analysing and Improving OCR Accuracy in Large Scale Historic Newspaper Digitisation Programs, *D-Lib Magazine* March/April 2009 Vol. 15, No. 3/4, ISSN 1082-9873.

IBM. (2003). Introduction to Grid Computing with Globus. *IBM RedBook*, URL: http://www.redbooks.ibm.com/redbooks/pdfs/sg246895.pdf, September 2003.

Khemakhem, M. et Belghith, A. (2009). Towards A Distributed Arabic OCR Based on the DTW Algoriyhm: Performance Analysis, *The International Arab Journal of Information Technology*, Vol. 6, No. 2, pp. 153-161, April 2009.

Khemakhem, M. et Belghith, A. (2009). A P2p Grid Architecture For Distributed Arabic OCR Based On The DTW Algorithm, *The International Journal of Computers and Applications (IJCA)*, Vol. 31.,No. 1, ACTA PRESS, 2009.

Khemakhem, M. & Belghith, A. (2007). Agent based architecture for Parallel and Distributed Complex Information Processing, *the International Revue on Computers and Softwares (IRECOS)*, Vol. 2, No. 1, January, 2007, 38–44.

Khemakhem, M.& Belghith, A. (2005). A Multipurpose Multi-Agent System based on a loosely coupled Architecture to speedup the DTW algorithm for Arabic printed cursive OCR, *Proceedings of the ACS/IEEE 2005 International Conference on Computer Systems and Applications*, pp. 121-vii, ISBN, Egypt, January 2005, aiccsa, Cairo

Khemakhem, M. Belghith, A.& Ben Ahmed,M. (1993). Modélisation architecturale de la Comparaison Dynamique distribuée, *Proceedings of the Second International Congress On Arabic and Advanced Computer Technology*, Casablanca, Morocco, December 1993.

Kumar, A. Balasubramanian, A. Namboodiri, AM.& Jawahar, C. (2006). Model-Based Annotation of Online Handwritten Datasets, *Proceedings of the Tenth International Workshop on Frontiers in Handwriting Recognition*, http://hal.inria.fr/inria-00105158/en/, 2006.

Philip, G. Bradford, (1992). Efficient Parallel Dynamic Programming, *Proceedings of the 30th Annual Allerton Conference on Communication, Control and Computing*, 185-194, University of Illinois, 1992.

Shi, Z. Huang, H. Luo, J. Lin, F.& Zhang, H.(2006). Agent Based Grid Computing, *Journal of Applied Mathematical Modelling*, Vol. 30, pp. 629-640 2006

Tapia,E.& Rojas, R. (2007). A Survey on Recognition of On-Line Handwritten Mathematical Notation *Technical Report B-07-01 Freie University at Berlin, Institut fur Informatik Takustr.*, 9, 14195 Berlin, Germany, January 26, 2007.

Vinciarelli, A.(2002). A survey on offline cursive word recognition, *Pattern Recognition*, Vol. 35, pp: 1433-1446, 2002.

Vuori, V. Laaksonen, J. Oja, E. et Kangas, J.(2001). Experiments with adaptation strategies for a prototype-based recognition system for isolated handwritten characters, *IJDAR*, Vol. 3, pp: 150-159, 2001.

6

Application of Gaussian-Hermite Moments in License

Lin Wang, Xinggu Pan, ZiZhong Niu and Xiaojuan Ma
Guizhou University for Nationalities
China

1. Introduction

In recent years, many researches on intelligent transportation systems (ITS) have been reported. ITSs are made up of 16 types of technology-based systems divided into intelligent infrastructure systems and intelligent vehicle systems. As one form of ITS technology, vehicle license plate recognition (VLPR) is one of important techniques that can be used for the identification of vehicles all over the world. There are many applications such as entrance admission, security, parking control, airport or harbor cargo control, road traffic control, speed control, toll gate automation and so on. LPR, as a means of vehicle identification, may be further exploited in various ways such as vehicle model identification, under-vehicle surveillance, speed estimation, and intelligent traffic management. Character recognition is an essential and important step in an ALPR system, which influences the overall accuracy and processing speed of the whole system significantly (Jia, 2007 & Christos-Nikolaos et al., 2008).

However, few researches have been done for recognition of car plate character. Neural network method has been employed to recognize car plate characters. The method can achieve promising performance if the quality of the given car plate image is well. However, the quality of image taken for car plates is not always well. This is due to the operating conditions (e.g. dust on the car plates) and distortion or degraded because of poor photographical environment. Experiments have shown that it is difficult to achieve high car plate recognition rates only by extracting features from character are fed into neural network method (Rosenfeld, 1969, Huang et al., 2008).

Moments, such as geometric moments and orthogonal moments, are widely used in pattern recognition, image processing, computer vision and multiresolution analysis (Shen, 1997, 2000; Wu & Shen, 2004; Wang et al., 2004, 2007;). We present in this paper a study on Gaussian-Hermite moments (GHMs), their calculation, properties, application and so forth.

In this paper, we at first the plate image by preprocessing algorithms (skew corrected, character segmentation, binary image and normalized) before recognition. Then, we propose the GHMs features as the input vector of BP neural network. Our analysis shows orthogonal moment's base functions of different orders having different number of zero crossings and very different shapes, therefore they can better reflect image features based on different modes, which is very interesting for pattern analysis, shape classification, and detection of the moving objects. Moreover, the base functions of GHMs are much more smoothed; are thus less sensitive to noise and avoid the artifacts introduced by window function's discontinuity (Fernandez-Garcia, & Medina-Carnicer 2004). Our method can have potential applications in video retrieval, and in other related areas of video information processing.

This paper is organized as follows. First, Section II introduces methods for image preprocessing. Section III presents the orthogonal Gaussian-Hermite moments and their behaviors in the license plate character image. In Section IV, proposes the GHMs features as the input vector of BP neural network for recognizing characters. Section V shows some experiment results. Finally, conclusions are drawn and with the future work discussed as well.

2. Image preprocessing

2.1 Orientation method for skew correction

The skew correction of license plate is an important step in ALPR. The license plate inclination is determined by the direction of the boundary. In order to find such direction. In our paper (Ma et al., 2009), the license plate image is firstly divided into a set of 5×5 non-overlapping blocks. The local orientation of each block is estimated by gradients [Gx,Gy] of pixels in the block. It may reduce much processing time. Next, the direction histogram which can reveal the overall orientation information in the license plate image is counted. The skew angle of license plate is detected by the local maximum of the direction histogram. This approach can solve the direction detection problem in a very straightforward and robust way under various conditions. Fig. 1 gives some images before and after skew correction.

Original images Adjusted images

Fig. 1. Corrected license plates

2.2 Segmentation character

This part extracts individual character images from the plate image. The plate window region can contain license surrounding some region that can create resistance in character recognition segment. In order to better extracte characters of plate image. We have to remove this unexpected region so that the image only holds the license number. This can be done by a horizontal segmentation and a vertical segmentation on both sides of the number plate. After segmenting horizontally and vertically, the plate image will be as the Fig. 2(c).

(a) (b) (c)

Fig. 2. Frame removal: (a) Original image; (b) The horizontal cut lines after corrected; (c) Frame removed

Then, calculating for segmentation points by the vertical projection and merging fragments that belong to the same character. The average filter with length s=3 reduce noise. The characters will be extracted from the vertical projection histogram of plate image. The extracted characters are given in Fig. 3.

2.3 Adaptive threshold for image binarization

All the character images are binarized using an anto-adaptive threshold. We propose many iterations algorithm for obtaining the optimal thresholds for segmenting gray scale images. The image background is black (gray value is 0) and the characters are white (gray value is 255).

Given that F(x,y) is the edge image and T is a predefined threshold Tn is a dynamic threshold. The following equation is used to obtain a local optimal threshold value.

$$\mathrm{T} = \frac{1}{2}\{\min[F(x,y)] + \max[F(x,y)]\} \tag{1}$$

$$\mathrm{T}_n = \frac{1}{2}\left[\frac{1}{M}\sum_{F(x,y)\le T}\sum F(x,y) + \frac{1}{N}\sum_{F(x,y)>T}\sum F(x,y)\right] \tag{2}$$

where M is number of pixel with its gray value less than T , N is number of pixel with its gray value larger than T.

<u>Loop :</u>
if ($T \approx T_n$)
    end loop;
else if | T- T_n | <0.6,
    T=T_n; goto loop;
end if

If the intensity of every pixel value is greater than T, the pixel is set to white; otherwise, it is set to black. The binary image is given in Fig. 3.

2.4 Normalization

Characters segmented from different car plates have different sizes. A linear normalization algorithm is applied to the input image to adjust to a uniform size.In our implementation, character blocks are normalized to a fixed size of 32*16 pixels.Assume the horizontal and vertical projections of the original image F be H and V, respectively. The normalization position (m,n) of (i,j) is obtained by

$$m = \sum_{k=1}^{i} H(k) \times \frac{M}{\sum_{k=1}^{j} H(k)} \tag{3}$$

$$n = \sum_{k=1}^{j} V(k) \times \frac{N}{\sum_{k=1}^{j} V(k)} \tag{4}$$

where m, n is height and width of normalized image.

Fig. 3. Character images before (upper) and after(lower) size normalization

3. Gaussian-Hermite moments (GHMs) and their behaviors in plate character

Moments, such as geometric moments and orthogonal moments, are widely used in pattern recognition, image processing, computer vision and multiresolution analysis. However, some moments base functions exhibit a great discontinuity [6] at the window boundary. In order to better represent local characteristics of images, particularly for noisy images, one should use orthogonal moments with a smoothing window function. Taking the well-known Gaussian functions as smoothing kernel, smoothed orthogonal Gaussian-Hermite moments (GHMs) were proposed [7-10]. Moreover, the base functions of GHMs are much more smoothed than other moments, thus less sensitive to noise and avoid the artifacts introduced by window function's discontinuity.

3.1 Gaussian-Hermite Moments

GHMs were proposed by J. Shen[11-12]. Given the Gaussian smoothing function $g(x,\sigma)$ with

$$g(x,\sigma) = (2\pi\sigma^2)^{-1/2} \exp(-x^2 / 2\sigma^2) \tag{5}$$

the nth order smoothed GHMs $M_n(x,S(x))$ of a signal $S(x)$ is defined as

$$M_n(x,S(x)) = \int_{-\infty}^{\infty} B_n(t) S(x+t) dt \qquad n = 0,1,2,\ldots \tag{6}$$

With

$$B_n(t) = g(t,\sigma) P_n(t) \tag{7}$$

Where $P_n(t)$ is a scaled Hermite polynomial function of order n defined by

$$P_n(t) = H_n(t/\sigma) \tag{8}$$

With

$$H_n(t/\sigma) = (-1)^n \exp(t^2)(d^n/dt^n)\exp(-t^2) \tag{9}$$

The GHMs can be recursively calculated as follows [10]:

$$M_n\left(x, S^{(m)}(x)\right) = 2(n-1)M_{n-2}\left(x, S^{(m)}(x)\right) + 2\sigma M_{n-1}\left(x, S^{(m+1)}(x)\right) \quad \text{for } m \geq 0 \text{ and } n \geq 2 \tag{10}$$

with

$$M_0\left(x, S^{(m)}(x)\right) = g(x,\sigma) * S^{(m)}(x) \qquad \text{for } m \geq 0 \tag{11}$$

$$M_1\left(x, S^{(m)}(x)\right) = 2\sigma d[g(x,\sigma)]/dx * S^{(m)}(x) \tag{12}$$

and in particular,

$$M_0(x, S(x)) = g(x,\sigma) * S(x) \tag{13}$$

$$M_1(x, S(x)) = 2\sigma d[g(x,\sigma) * S(x)]/dx \tag{14}$$

Where

$$S^m(x) = d^m S(x)/dx^m \tag{15}$$

$$S^0(x) = S(x) \tag{16}$$

and * denotes the convolution operator.

Now we analyze the spatial domain behavior of smoothed GHMs base functions. Because the nth order Hermite polynomial $H_n(t)$ has n different real roots, the base function of GHMs $g(x,\sigma)H_n(x/\sigma)$ will also have n different real roots. Therefore the base function of the nth order GHMs will change its sign n times. In other words, it consists of n oscillations. So GHMs can well characterize different spatial modes as other orthogonal moments. Fig. 4 shows the spatial behavior of GHMs base functions of different orders.

As to the frequency domain behavior, since Gaussian-Hermite base functions comprise more and more oscillations when the order n is increased, they will thus contain more and more high frequencies. From the spectral analysis viewpoint, the GHMs efficiently separate the signal features in different frequency bands. Fig. 5 shows the Fourier transform amplitude of some base functions of GHMs.

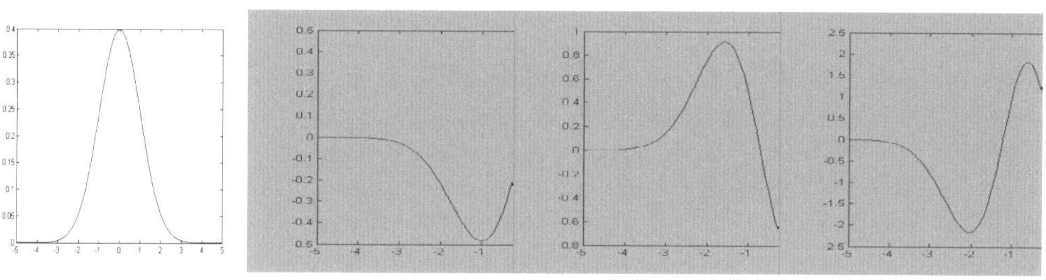

Fig. 4. Spatial behavior of 1D GHMs base functions (orders: 0 to 3)

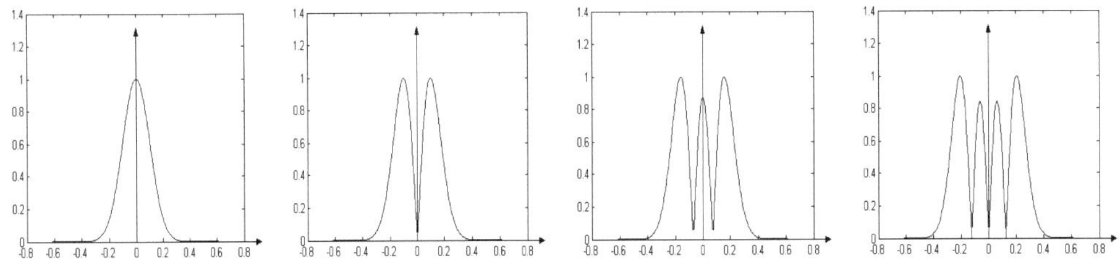

Fig. 5. Frequency behavior of 1D GHMs base functions (orders: 0 to 3)

Moreover, from the recursive calculation of GHMs, we see that these moments are in fact linear combinations of the derivatives of the signal filtered by a Gaussian filter. As is well known, the derivatives have been extensively used for image representation in pattern recognition.

2D orthogonal Gaussian-Hermite moments of order (p,q) of an input image $I(x,y)$ can be defined similarly

$$M_{p,q} = \iint_{-\infty}^{\infty} G(t,v,\sigma) H_{p,q}(t/\sigma, v/\sigma) S(x+t, y+t) dtdv \tag{17}$$

Where $G(t,v,\sigma)$ is the 2D Gaussian function, and $H_{p,q}(t/\sigma, v/\sigma)$, the scaled 2D Hermite polynomial of order (p,q) , with

$$H_{p,q}(t/\sigma, v/\sigma) = H_p(t/\sigma) H_q(v/\sigma) \tag{18}$$

Obviously, 2D Gaussian-Hermite moments are separable, so the recursive algorithm in 1D cases can be applied for their calculation. Fig. 6 shows the Fourier transform amplitude of a bidimensional GHMs kernels of different orders. We use GHMs to efficiently recognition the character plate image.

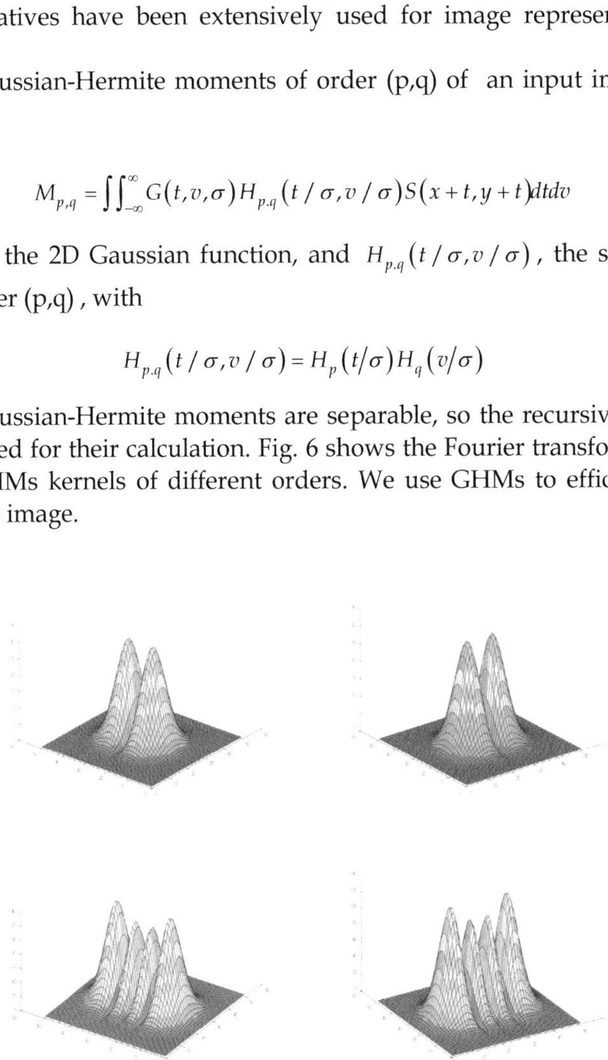

Fig. 6. Frequency behavior of 2D base functions of GHMs (orders: (0,1), (1, 0), (0, 3) and (3, 0))

3.2 Representation of feature vector with of GHMs in license plate character

In order to characterize these features in the license plate character image, we use 231 2D base functions of GHMs of different order (orders: $p+q \leq 20$). The number and the order of GHMs required were empirically determined.

The feature vector with Gaussian-Hermite moments $M_{p,q}$ of license plate character is represented by

$$M = [M_{0,0}, M_{0,1}, M_{0,2}, \dots, M_{0,20}, \quad M_{1,1}, \dots, M_{1,19}, \dots, \; M_{19,0}, M_{19,1}, \; M_{20,0}]^T \quad (19)$$

4. Character recognition

For the recognition of segmented characters, the Gaussian-Hermite moments features are extracted from each character are lumped into a vector as input of the BP neural network [13,14]. The Bp neural network is a three-layer structure.

4.1 BPNN model

A neural network (NN) is an artificial network model, which emulates the cerebral nerve network in the brain. Characters are recognized using a supervised back propagation neural network (BPNN) classifier (see Fig.7). A BPNN is trained by adjusting the weights of the connections between the nodes of the different layers before the BPNN can be used. The input patterns are fed into the input layer and the error between the expected output and the actual output are propagated backwards through the network such that the weights can be adjusted to minimize the errors. This training procedure is repeated until the error is sufficiently small. When learning of neural network complete, we can used that for recognize character of license plate. A major advantage of BPNN is that a trained network is capable of classifying unknown pattern with little computational effort. In this paper, we use a three-layered BPNN architecture. Fig. 7 shows the three-layered BP neural network architecture.

4.2 Input of BPNN with GHMs features

The Gaussian-Hermite moments feature obtained from license plate character as the input vector of BPNN. We use GHMs feature extraction as our method for character recognition. Since the base functions of GHMs are much more smoothed and thus less sensitive to noise, GHMs could facilitate the recognition of character in noisy image sequences. This method distinguishes characters by their unique features.

The license plate character images is characterized by a vector of Gaussian-Hermite moment Mp+q (in our experiment, $\sigma = 0.6$). The order of used moments are of 0th-20th (N = 20).

The character images (including references and noisy images) is then characterized by 231 2D moments of orders (0,0),(0,1),...,(0.20), (1,0), (1,1) ,..., (1,19),...,(20,0).

The number of units in BPNN is shown in Table 1. The three-layered BPNN that contains 231 input units, 120 hidden units. Learning rate was 0.05, and the number of learning cycles was 5000, an error value less than 1.0*10-7, then learning stopped. It has 34 types of characters, including 24 character and 10 numbers, the maximum sample number for training and testing is 200.

The number of units in BPNN

Input layer	231
Hidden layer	120
Output layer	6

Table 1.

We use Network to denote the number and character network. According to the feature of Network, 6 neurons are set. So the output vector is $O=[o_1,o_2,o_3,o_4,o_5,o_6,]$, the expectation output of network is {0,0,0,0,0,0}, {0,0,0,0,0,1}, {0,0,0,0,1,0}, {0,0,0,0,1,1},..., {0,1,1,1,1,1}, {1,0,0,0,0,0}, {1,0,0,0,0,1} corresponds number and character separately.
The number of hidden neurons relates to the input and output unit directly. If the hidden neurons are too few, the network possibly cannot train well, local minimum are more and no robust, it could not distinguish the sample which had not seen before, and the fault tolerance is bad. The increase hidden neurons maybe improve the match precision between the network and the training set, but it will causes the study time too long again, the error is also uncertain the best. The choice of hidden neurons is given according to the empirical formula usually:

$$n=\sqrt{n_1 n_0}+\delta(1\le\delta\le 10) \tag{20}$$

n1, n0 are the number of inputs and the output respectively, so the neural network structure is shown as Fig.7.

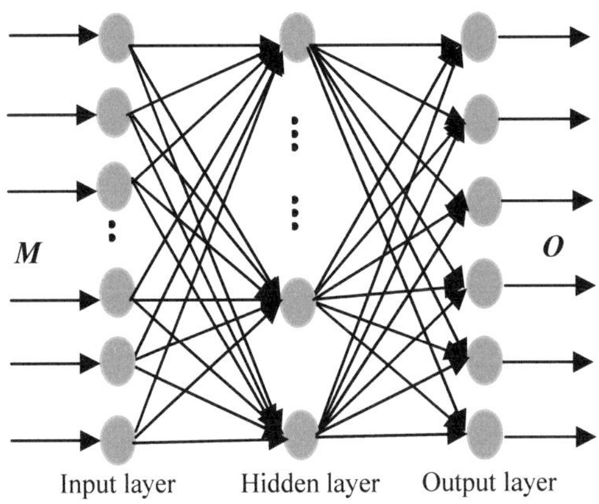

Fig. 7. Three layers BPNN Structure

5. Experimental result

In this section, preliminary experiments for testing the feasibility and robustness of our method are conducted by applying the above-mentioned procedure. One is license plate images which are directly captured by a mobile surveillance system. There are 200 training and testing sample images to be processed using our algorithm. Table 2 shows the results using this set of images.
The testing results using the images in the first category are very encouraging. The average recognition accuracy is 97.93%. Among 200 testing images, only few very poorly focused samples have failed for the number of character training samples is not many. The increase

of training samples would improve recognition accuracy. As a whole, these results are satisfactory enough for the character recognition process.

Correctness Rate (%) / Input of BPNN	Character	Uppercase	Number
proposed feature (Pan et al., 2005)	86.7	89.2	87.4
GHMs feature	98.6	97.4	97.8

Table 2. Experimental results

6. Conclusion and future work

Although significant progress has been made in the last decade, there is still work to be done, as a robust LP recognition system should effectively work for a variety of environmental illumination, plate types/conditions, as well as acquisition parameters. Moreover, most LPR systems focus on the processing of images with one vehicle. Nevertheless, input images may contain more than one vehicle or motorcycles.

In addition, assuming that LP regions are detectable even in very low resolution, an open topic for future research is the readability improvement of LP text using image processing techniques. Research for improving degraded plates has lately been directed to superresolution methods for video sequences or to blurred plate images with promising results.

Though the new method proposed in this paper is still in its stage of a prototype, it has already shown its potential for various implementations. This method can also be used for detecting the moving objects. Our research will be carried on following this track.

7. Acknowledgment

The work was supported by the National Natural Science Foundation of China (No. 60965001) and The Guizhou Key Laboratory of Pattern Recognition and Intelligent System.

8. References

Jia, W.; Zhang, H. & He, X. (2007). Region-based license plate detection. *Journal of Network and Computer Applications*, Vol. 30, 2007, pp. 1324-1333, ISSN: 1084-8045

Rosenfeld, A. (1969). Picture Processing by Computer. *Academic Press*, New York, 1969, ISBN: ISBN: 0-12-597350-0

Huang, Y.P.; Chang, T.W. Chen, Y.R & Sandnes, F.E. (2008). A back propagation based real-time license plate recognition system. *International Journal of Pattern Recognition and Artificial Intelligence*, vol. 22, no. 2, pp.233-251, 2008, ISSN: 0218-0014

Christos-Nikolaos, E.; Loannis, E. & Loannis, D. (2008). License Plate Recogniton From Still Images and Video Sequences: A Survey. *IEEE Transaction on Intelligent Transportation Systems*, Vol.9, no.3, 2008. ISSN: 1524-9050

Shen, J. (1997). Orthogonal Gaussian-Hermite Moments for Image Characterization. *Proc. Intelligent Robots and Computer Vision XVI: Algorithms Techniques, Active Vision, and*

Materials Handling, pp.224-233, ISBN: 0-8194-2640-7, Pittsburgh, USA, 15-17, Oct. 1997

Shen, J.; Shen, W. & Shen, D. (2000). On Geometric and orthogonal moments. *International Journal of Pattern Recognition and Artificial Intelligence*, Vol.14 (7), 2000, pp.875-894, ISSN: 0218-0014

Wu, Y. & Shen, J. (2004). Moving object detection using orthogonal Gaussian-Hermite moments. *Visual communication and image processing*, Vol.5308, 2004, pp.841-849, ISBN: 9780819452115

Wang, L.; Dai, M. & Geng, G.H. (2004). Fingerprint Image Segmentation by Energy of Gaussian-Hermite Moments. *Sinobiometrics 2004*, vol. 3338 of Lecture Notes Comput.Sci., pp.414-423, 2004. ISBN: 978-3-540-24029-7, Springer-Verlag.

Wang, L. & Dai, M. (2007). Application of New Type of Singular Points in Fingerprint Classification. *Pattern Recognition Letter*, vol.28，2007, pp.1640-1650, ISSN:0167-8655

Fernandez-Garcia, N.L. & Medina-Carnicer, R. (2004). Characterization of empirical discrepancy evaluation measures, *Pattern Recognition Letters*, Vol.25(1), 2004, pp.35-47, ISSN:0167-8655

Ma, X.; Pan, R. & Wang, L. (2009). A Method Based on Orientation Field for Skew Correction of License Plate. *2009 Asia-Pacific Conference on Computational Intelligence and Industrial Applications*, pp. 308-311, ISBN: 978-1-4244-4606-3, Wuhan, China, 28-29 Nov. 2009

Pan, X.; Ye, X. & Zhang S.Y. (2005). A hybrid method for robust car plate character recognition. *Engineering Applications of Artificial Intelligence*, Vol.18, 2005, pp. 963-972, ISSN: 1062-922X